# StarWalker and the Fairy Queen

Alyson Budde

Pick-a-Woo Woo

Pick-a-Woo Woo

**Copyright © 2014**
The right of Alyson Budde to be identified as the Author and DeeDee Draz Barreras to be identified as the Cover Artist of the work has been asserted by them in accordance with the Copyright, Designs and Patents Act 1988.
All rights reserved. No part of this book may be used or reproduced, stored in a retrieval system, or transmitted in any form, or by any means electronic, mechanical, recording, photocopying, or in any manner whatsoever without

**National Library of Australia Cataloguing-in-Publication entry**
Author:     Budde, Alyson, author.
Title:       Star Walker and the Fairy Queen / Alyson Budde (author).
ISBN:      9781921883552 (paperback)
Series:     Budde, Alyson. Fairies in space; 1.
Target Audience: For primary school age.
Subjects:  Fairies--Juvenile fiction.
           Outer space--Juvenile fiction.
Dewey Number: A823.4

**Title:** Star Walker and the Fairy Queen
**Book Description:** In a single act of bad fairy magic by her brother, Iliyan (the Fairy Queen) is hopelessly lost and left, utterly without memory, in space. Rescued by StarWalker, healed and helped by a family of shaman dragons, Iliyan's memory is restored, but the location of her home remains unknown. A journey to the Fairy Star initiates a series of foretold events that reveal Iliyan's mysterious epic destiny. Meanwhile, on Earth, Nib (an elf) and his gnome friend, Mc*Manigal, stumble into mounting fairy chaos and choose to act to save the Fairy Glen. In Inner Earth, they navigate the treacherous Crystal River rapids, pass the Wizard's three tests, locate the Inner Earth library, find the Queen's missing brother and journey to the heart of Inner Earth to retrieve a critical piece of the puzzle of Iliyan's disappearance.

*StarWalker and the Fairy Queen* is about guts, collaboration, and friendship. In the face of harrowing circumstances, each is tested and revealed a hero. Monumental and Earth-changing magic results from the journey. And none of them could have done it alone.

**Publishing Details:**
Published in Australia - Pick-A-Woo Woo Publishers
www.pickawoowoo.com

**Printed:**
Lightning Source (US / UK/ EUR/ AUS)
**Distributed**
Ingram Book Group, Baker & Taylor and more (US/UK/EUR/ AUS)

**Books Available through:**
Ingram www.ingrambook.com
Amazon.com www.amazon.com
Baker & Taylor www.btol.com
Barnes & Noble www.barnesandnoble.com
Amazon.com www.amazon.uk
Bertrams www.bertrams.com
Book Depository Ltd www.bookdepository.co.uk
Pick-a-Woo Woo books can be found in bookstores and online stores worldwide. If you are unable to order any of the Pick-a-Woo Woo Publishers children's books locally, please contact us at info@pickawoowoo.com and we will locate your nearest retailer or an online store.

# Acknowledgements

My greatest gratitude for the love and inspiration from my family – Steve and Ethan Budde, Claire Jadulang, Valerie and Jim Garrott, Susan and David Dameron, and Dena and Wil Prim; from my sisterhood – Marilyn Helgeson, Stephanie Reynolds, Lori Bertazzon, Laura Walthers, Kana Koinuma, April Jackson, Margaret Hope, Tanya Danser, Joanne Matulich, and Carrie Barber; from the wizards who were my teachers – Bill Perkiss, Elizabeth P. Morse, Peggy Rubin and Jean Houston; from the players of Wonderland Playhouse – Lily Bouse, Lauren Beebe, Joey Chadwick, Jessica Bazan, and Madison Scheafer; from wordsmiths Julie-Ann Harper and Wendy McQueen; from Jill and Richard Dominguez for their act of rescuing Luke and giving him to us; from DeeDee Draz Barreras who, although she never met him, depicted him perfectly, and to Iliyan and StarWalker for sharing their story with me.

For anyone who has ever loved a dog.

# Contents

Acknowledgements ........................................................... 3

Chapter 1: The Fairly Dusty Moon ................................. 7

Chapter 2: Nib's Choice ...................................................... 12

Chapter 3: The Dragon World ......................................... 24

Chapter 4: The Wizard's Cavern ...................................... 37

Chapter 5: The Fairy Star ................................................... 54

Chapter 6: Prince Kelm ...................................................... 70

Chapter 7: Gaia's Wish ........................................................ 88

Chapter 8: The Abandonment ......................................... 98

Chapter 9: Going Deeper ................................................... 107

Chapter 10: The Dying Star ............................................... 118

Chapter 11: Sacred Geometry ........................................... 125

Chapter 12: Return to Earth ............................................. 132

About the Author ................................................................ 139

# Chapter 1

# The Fairly Dusty Moon

When she awoke, Iliyan didn't know she was a victim of fairy magic. She rubbed her eyes. Dim red light surrounded her. She sat on the fairly dusty surface of an unknown world. As far as she could see there was nothing and no one, just dust and a few boulders. No plants grew. Faint light from a distant sun cast a red glow across the surface. Iliyan's short flowered dress glowed red too.

*What good is a dress in a place like this*, she thought. She was glad she had boots on. She brushed some dust from her dress and stood up to go exploring. Pain gripped her and she fell back to the ground. Iliyan was sure she couldn't walk.

A small paper sack sat on the ground beside her. Inside she found some plums. *Odd*, she thought. She took a bite, but she wasn't hungry.

This was a fine mess. Here she was. Well, where was she exactly? And why was there no one else around? She wondered if she were dreaming. She sifted dry, gritty, red dirt through her fingers. This was not a dream. Although she wasn't really scared, Iliyan didn't like being alone, so she did the only thing she could think to do. She put her head on her knees and she cried.

StarWalker snacked. He had leaped to a small planet where he'd found some cheese. He was pleased. Cheese was his favorite snack.

Thoroughly distracted by sparkling lights, StarWalker spent his time leaping through space. He leaped from stars to planets, planets to asteroids, and asteroids to comets. He could leap great, long distances. He had visited many worlds and had met many interesting beings, and because he was a dog, he was loved by all of them.

*I must remember this place when I get hungry.* He strained. StarWalker could never remember where he'd been. Efforts to map his routes frustrated him. With one exception, if he wanted to return to a place he simply had to wait until he happened upon it. The exception was the Dragon World where his best friend lived. StarWalker would hold a picture of Aneurin in his mind like a target and he would leap directly to the Dragon World. It always worked, but it didn't work with cheese. StarWalker didn't know why.

In addition to his great strong legs, StarWalker had super-sonic hearing. Years later, when he was an old dog, StarWalker would say that up until the day he met Iliyan, he had never before heard the sound of crying. So, when he first became aware of it he had no idea what it was. He only knew it sounded sad and far away. And even though it is difficult to imagine a dog would leave a place where there was cheese, StarWalker felt his legs crouch and the next thing he knew he leaped toward the crying sound. He touched off three planets in a row and landed on a star. The sound grew louder. His final leap was to the red moon of a planet he had never visited before.

Following the sound, he nearly tripped over Iliyan who was exactly where we left her (head on her knees, with her plums in the sack beside her). StarWalker nudged her and she looked up into clear golden eyes. His white fur twinkled like starlight. He cocked his head to the side. Great floppy ears with freckles hung from the sides of his broad head. He had a large golden freckle over his left eye and one in the center of the top of his head. He stood tall. With the dog standing and Iliyan sitting, the two were face to face. Iliyan was so relieved to have some company she wasn't even startled.

'Who are you?' She felt his soft ears.

StarWalker's lips never moved, but Iliyan clearly heard his response in her head. StarWalker was telepathic.

*'I am StarWalker. Why are you making that sound?'*

'I'm crying because I'm sad.'

*'Why are you sad?'*

'Because I'm all alone and I don't know where I am.'

StarWalker thought this an odd thing to be concerned about. He was often surprised by where he found himself, but he was never concerned about where he was.

*'You are here. What is your name?'*

Iliyan thought for a moment. 'I don't know that either.' She knew she had a name, but it was as if no one had ever told her what it was. 'I can't remember anything. It's as if I've appeared for the first time in this dusty place.'

StarWalker knew at once that something was wrong. He knew that one did not appear in a place, one leaped there. Although he understood not being able to remember things, he had never forgotten his name. He knew that while he may not be able to remember how to get back to the cheese planet, he would remember that he'd been there and that he'd found cheese. It would be unfortunate not to remember it at all.

*'I will sit with you.'* StarWalker circled and settled down in the red dirt.

*Alyson Budde*

Iliyan rested her head on StarWalker's back while he told her stories of his adventures. His favorite was the time he landed on the peewee planet. All the beings there were the size of the end of his nose. They had never seen a dog before. He so impressed them that they organized a festival in his honor. Hundreds of peewees carried him on a mat down a path lined with many more cheering and hollering peewees. They placed him on a stone pedestal and sang songs to him. He was overwhelmed. A few peewees with special robes approached him and spoke many words he didn't understand. They offered him tiny food, which he enjoyed. He felt special. Then he heard something, or maybe he saw a twinkling light. StarWalker couldn't remember what caught his attention, but before he knew it he crouched and leaped, leaving the peewees behind. He had not seen them since that day.

*'Hey! You could go leaping with me!'*

'But I can't walk. I have this terrible pain in my stomach.'

*'You must have hurt yourself when you landed here.'* StarWalker sniffed Iliyan. *'The first time I leaped to the Dragon World I landed badly and broke my leg. I couldn't walk. Aneurin found me and flew me to his home. His dad is a medicine dragon and he fixed my leg. I stayed there a long time and they took care of me. I'll bet his dad could help you.'*

Iliyan shook her head. StarWalker was large and he looked strong, but she wasn't sure he could carry her.

*'I am a strong dog.'* StarWalker stood broadly with his chest puffed out. *'If you can climb up and hold on, I believe I can carry you.'*

Iliyan looked at the Fairly Dusty Moon. If she didn't want to stay alone she would have to go with him. Two traveling space together seemed, to Iliyan, better than one staying alone. So, she grabbed her plums and climbed on StarWalker's back.

*'Hold on!'* StarWalker pictured Aneurin in his mind. In the picture, Aneurin was playing with potions in his father's laboratory. StarWalker had sat many hours and watched his friend at work in the lab. Satisfied that the picture of his friend was clear, he crouched low and leaped to a star. StarWalker leaped again and landed on the dark side of a moon. Iliyan's eyes barely adjusted when StarWalker crouched again.

'This is fun.' Iliyan held on tight. 'Where is your home?'

*'This is it.'* StarWalker's ears flapped in the breeze.

'What do you mean? This is space.'

*'This is where I live. If I have a home, I can't remember where it is.'*

'Like me.' Iliyan buried her head in StarWalker's neck. 'Does it worry you?'

*'No. I love to leap. I get lucky. I meet folks. Before I met you, I found some cheese.'*

'Don't you get lonely?'

*'Yes. I'm glad I know Aneurin.'*

'Now you know me.' Iliyan squeezed StarWalker's neck. StarWalker felt warmth travel through his body.

## Chapter 2

# Nib's Choice

On Earth the fairies dithered. The Fairy Glen had fallen into disarray. Flowers wilted. Plants died. Ordinarily sparkling and clear, the lake oozed murky and brown. Flies hovered. The fairies had stopped working, and fairies never stop working. They do need to be told what to do, however, and that's the Fairy Queen's job. The problem was, the Fairy Queen had gone missing.

A pulsing buzz filled the air. It grew louder, then faded, grew louder still, then faded again. It throbbed the growing panic of hundreds of fairies who fluttered back and forth, one to another, asking, 'Have you seen her?'

Nearby in the forest, Nib (an elf) was distracted from his arrows game. 'What is that noise?' he huffed to his frog companion.

'Ribbit,' was its only response.

Nib shot another arrow. It missed its mark. He stomped around. 'Well, this is impossible. I can't concentrate with all that noise.'

Arrows was a game Nib had invented to play when he was alone in the forest. He shot arrows at tree targets while blindfolded. It required keen focus of all of his senses, especially his hearing. Sometimes he spun himself dizzy to increase the challenge. His mother thought the game silly, which only made Nib want to play it more. On target about half the time, he practiced to improve his accuracy. Today, all his arrows missed their marks.

'Darn!' Nib collected his arrows. The din from the Fairy Glen grew louder. He decided to investigate.

The Fairy Glen sat on the edge of the forest just beyond the Elfin Village. Nib visited there when his mother needed herbs or honey. The Glen was usually quiet. Often, he had to play tricks to find a fairy. Fairies adore games and mischief, but they love their plants above all things and would never neglect them. Even before he reached the Glen, Nib saw abandoned plants grown wild and fallen over. Dead branches and flower petals littered the forest floor.

Chaos met Nib as he stepped out of the forest. Gobs of fairies flew willy-nilly from tree to bush to flower, bumping into one another, their alarm mounting. The sight of hysterical fairies worried Nib. No good could come from this fairy confusion. He stuck out his hand. A boy fairy landed in the center of his palm.

'Who are you?' Nib asked.

'I am Kopo.'

'What's going on here?'

'The Queen and her brother, Prince Kelm, have disappeared. Do you know where they are?'

'No. How long have they been gone?'

'Two days.' Kopo's voice sounded shrill. 'We don't know what to do.'

'I can see that.'

Kopo flew away. Nib thought hard. He didn't know what to do. He thought about his elf friends, but none of them knew anything about fairies. Maybe he was supposed to help. After all, he was the one who wandered into this mess. His mother often said the one who helped was the one who showed up. The problem was that Nib didn't know how to help. He felt stupid. He nearly walked away because he felt so unsure.

Elves are Earth creatures. They live in Inner Earth and on the surface. Unlike fairies, who have specific plant tending duties, elves are general helpers. When help is needed elves always say, 'Yes!' They love the Earth, her mountains and meadows, her waterways, her night sky, her magical creatures, her birds and animals, and they love her dirt. Elves are not dreamers. They don't suffer wanderlust or spend their time wishing they were someplace else. An elf can live its entire life in the same place. Earth is home, and home is enough to an elf.

Nib knew that if the Fairy Queen never returned, the fairies would forget where they lived and stray away. If they strayed away, the Earth would suffer. The Glen would no longer be a place to play and Nib would always know he had been there the day everything changed. Order had to be restored to the Glen. Nib's heart reminded him how much he loved the Glen and in that moment he made a choice.

Nib walked into the fairy ring: a circle of old trees so tall their branches entwined overhead. Fairy celebrations took place there. During full moons, fairies gathered like fireflies and danced until dawn. Nib took his panpipes from his pocket and played his favorite song. The fairies assembled, unable to resist the sweet notes of Nib's pipes. Fairy sparks flew all about him.

'Listen!' Nib stuffed his pipes in his pant's pocket. 'I need your help. I need to talk to all the fairies, especially the Fay fairies.'

Fay fairies were the fairy elders. Unlike the small Glen fairies, Fays were very tall, and very recluse. They hid in the forest and it was nearly impossible to entice a Fay into conversation.

'Go into the forest and bring the Fay fairies here.' Nib hoped the small fairies could get the Fays' attention. 'I'll play my pipes until you return to remind you of your task. Don't get distracted. This is important. Once everyone is here I will reveal my plan to find the Queen.'

The small fairies scattered. Nib played his pipes and tried to think up a plan. Slowly the ring filled with forest beings of all kinds. Fairies, elves, gnomes and satyrs buzzed with news of the Queen's disappearance. Nib looked around hoping to gain some inspiration. At the ring's edge, he saw the Queen's cousins.

'Friends of the fields and forests, I bid you good day. Thank you for coming.' As he spoke, Nib recognized Eritha, the Queen's cousin. 'The Fairy Queen and Prince Kelm are missing. I plan to go straight away and try to find them. I know you are concerned, but you must get back to work. The Glen needs your attention.' He looked at Eritha. 'I wonder if Princess Eritha would take charge until the Queen's return.'

'I will do my best.' Eritha stepped into the ring. She was tall, with long brown hair and she moved like flowing water. Delighted, she immediately collected the small fairies. She made quick work of assigning each fairy to care for a plant. The job of choosing the right plant for each fairy was easier than she expected. She had watched her cousin do it before and had inquired about the process. The Queen told her that if one looked carefully at a small fairy, it was obvious which plant she belonged to. Eritha had been skeptical, but now she could see it was true. As Eritha worked, Nib watched the fairies return to their plants. The panicked buzz subsided.

Nib couldn't believe his good fortune, nor could he believe he alone was responsible for his quick success. Magic of unknown origin occurred often in the forest. One never knew who might be assisting from nearby. Nib was quick to acknowledge his good fortune.

'Great gratitude!' he said to the space around him. Choosing Princess Eritha had been a great idea. He marveled at how the idea had come to him. Just a moment before, he had been completely unsure what to do. He had been ready to walk away and leave the Glen to uncertain fate, but he changed his mind and somehow a great idea just came to him when he needed it. He was a lucky elf.

Satisfied the fairies were in good hands, Nib turned his attention to finding the Queen. He rounded up the elves, gnomes and satyrs. He needed clues. He had watched gnomes comb the Earth. They were very thorough and good at finding lost things. Nib considered how best to approach them. He didn't speak gnome and talking to them could be tricky. Gnomes speak elfin, but they can get snippy with folks who don't speak gnome. Nib decided to take a chance.

'Gnomes!' Nib cleared his throat. 'I need someone to comb the forest to look for clues. I have seen you work and there is no one better for this job. Can you help?' The gnomes looked first at Nib, then at each other. They nodded.

'Thank you.' Nib let out the breath he'd been holding. He was grateful and relieved. The combing began where each gnome stood. Slowly they worked their way through the Glen.

Nib sent the elves to the Elfin Village to quiz their neighbors. The satyrs he sent further out, past the boundaries of the forest. Nib spotted Mc*Manigal, one of the older gnomes he knew from the forest.

'Mc*Manigal, I need someone to go with me, someone stronger and more clever than I am.'

'I'd be honored. I would.' Mc*Manigal swelled. 'The Fairy Queen is a great friend of the gnomes.'

'I don't know how long we'll be gone,' said Nib.

'No matter.' Mc*Manigal adjusted his vest. 'Adventure knows no time.'

'I think we should go to Inner Earth and see the Wizard. Are you ready?'

'Always ready, Chief!' Mc*Manigal nodded and tipped his cap.

Nib and Mc*Manigal trotted out of the Fairy Glen and into the forest at a sprightly pace. One might think a gnome would have trouble keeping up with an elf twice his size, but gnomes are nimble and quick. Despite their size differences, Mc*Manigal and Nib ran into the forest side by side.

Nib headed for an immense elm tree. The tree actually looked like two trees attached together at their trunks, like Siamese trees. In fact, it was not two trees grown together, but one tree split apart by lightning during a storm. When one looked upon it at just the right angle, a slim doorway was visible in the trunk's split. This was an Inner Earth gate.

As they made for the gate, a tree faun stepped out from behind the tree. Nib and Mc*Manigal nearly collided they stopped so fast. Shaped like a goat with an elfin face, the faun was the palest shade of green. Its nose curved down to a point; its eyes curved up. The tips of its thin pointed ears reached nearly to the top of its head. Nib looked at the faun twice, as it appeared to disappear when viewed from certain angles. The faun was an Inner Earth gatekeeper.

While the faun examined them, Mc*Manigal slipped his hand inside the pocket of Nib's vest. Nib reached in to find three cool nuggets. The faun spoke with a high-pitched voice that echoed.

'Who desires to enter this portal?'

'It is I, Nib, and my friend Mc*Manigal. We come in service to the fairies. The Fairy Queen has gone missing. We must see the Wizard.'

'Give me the pass key!' the faun squeaked. Nib held out the nuggets. They shone bright gold. The faun took one in his mouth and bit down. Satisfied, the faun backed up, opened the gate and allowed the adventurers to pass. Out of nowhere the faun produced a torch. Nib took the torch as he crossed the gate threshold into a dark cave.

The torch filled the cave with light. They trekked deep inside. The cave emptied into a meadow. Nib and Mc*Manigal walked across the meadow and over a hill. The light grew brighter. It looks like dawn all the time in Inner Earth. It's not bright, but it's enough light to see by. Once their eyes adjusted, Nib dropped the torch and stomped out the fire.

'Do you hear the river?' Nib said.

'Barely,' said Mc*Manigal. 'It's still a ways off.'

'Not as far as you'd think.' Nib knew that distance was measured differently in Inner Earth. One might see a thing and think it very far off, then set out for it and arrive very quickly. Conversely, one might think a thing appears close by and find it takes forever to reach it. It was as if Earth always had the last laugh. It took some getting used to. Nib had learned to keep his eyes open and assume nothing when in Inner Earth.

They reached the river. The water moved swiftly. It looked dark and deep. They came upon a wooden rowboat. A black cat sat at the tiller. Nib spoke a few words in feline and stretched to scratch the cat's ears. The cat moved aside and Nib got in the boat. The cat hissed when he saw Mc*Manigal. Cats and gnomes are not famous friends.

'It's all right.' Nib stroked the cat. 'He's a pleasant little man once you get to know him.' The cat arched his back and rattled his tail. It was a cat warning.

'I got that.' Mc*Manigal backed up. 'I'll just get in at the front if that's okay.' He walked a wide path around to the front of the boat, pulled it into the river, and climbed in. Everyone settled down and Nib took the oars. The river grabbed the boat and thrust it in the direction of Crystal Lake.

Now, the Wizard's whereabouts is information that cannot be known. It must be discovered. One seeking the Wizard must row to the center of Crystal Lake, drop anchor, and announce his intentions as loudly and with as much heart as he can muster. The seeker must then await the Wizard's reply.

Nib rowed. The river was lively. It flowed deep into Inner Earth. Along its banks, crystals glowed turquoise, emerald, pink, yellow, purple and silver. Musical tones rang from each one. Together the tones formed a symphony that sang sweetly as Nib rowed by.

Farther down, the river grew spirited. The crystal symphony boomed unpleasant. Nib understood the change of tone to be a warning of danger ahead. He prepared himself. Presently, a particularly treacherous stretch of rapids began that nearly launched Nib into the water. Nib threw an oar to Mc*Manigal. 'Here, take an oar!'

They tried to row sitting down. Despite their attempts to navigate the boat down the river, it slammed into rocks that were hidden just beneath the water's surface. Each time they hit a rock, Nib and Mc*Manigal slid across the thwart and smashed violently into the hull.

'We should stand up.' Nib nearly toppled over in the boat. 'Stay low so you can shift your weight.' They used the oars to push the boat away

*Alyson Budde*

from the rocks. Still, they were jostled and thrown. The boat jumped, smacked and cracked.

'I wish we had a canoe.' Nib worried the boat might break apart.

'That would better?' Mc*Manigal smirked.

Nib felt his shoulders and legs tense up from crouching low in the boat. The muscles in his thighs burned.

'Stay loose or you'll end up swimming,' Nib yelled.

Growing tension in their muscles made it impossible to absorb the shock of the ride. Mc*Manigal whistled. Although his whistling was barely audible over the crashing crystal symphony and the fast-moving water, Nib appreciated the effort. It did calm him down.

The rapids continued unyielding. Unable to control his tension, pain overtook Nib's legs and back. He became nauseous. He thought he might vomit. 'Great!' he thought. 'Now I'm going to throw up.' He rowed as long as he could then he dropped the oar, clutched his stomach, and fell into the boat.

'Are you all right, Chief?' Mc*Manigal took Nib's oar. Nib put his head between his knees. Mc*Manigal shifted his weight, one oar in each hand. He poked at the river. The boat crashed along. Mc*Manigal held the boat as steady as he could. After a while the violence slowed. The crystal symphony hushed. The river calmed. Mc*Manigal sat next to Nib.

Nib looked up, sighed heavily, and laughed. He laughed long and loud. Mc*Manigal laughed too. A moment later Nib felt better. He stood up. He was amazed he hadn't vomited. He hated vomiting. His relief grew passionate as he yelled out to the space around him.

'Great Gratitude!' He was grateful for the crystal's symphonic warning. He was grateful the boat hadn't capsized and that no one was launched overboard. He was grateful he hadn't had to fish his traveling companions out of the rapids. He didn't know if gnomes could swim. He knew cats could swim, but he'd seen a wet cat before. A soaking wet, raging ball of claws and teeth was a lousy boat mate. He was truly grateful the rapids were behind them. He did an elf dance in the center of the boat and retrieved his oar from Mc*Manigal.

'Settle down, Sparky!' Mc*Manigal laughed. 'Haven't you had enough excitement?'

'Just glad we got through it. I'm so glad I didn't vomit.'

'You and me both, Chief!'

'Take a break, Mac!'

'Don't mind if I do.' Mc*Manigal relaxed in the boat. Carried along by the rock symphony, Nib settled into a rowing rhythm. Before long, the river widened where Crystal Lake began. Nib pointed the boat at the lake's center and rowed on. Once there he dropped anchor, stood up and cleared his throat.

'Wizard! It's me, Nib, from the Elfin Village. I need your help. The Fairy Queen and her brother have gone missing and the Fairy Glen is in a terrible state. I have left one of the Fay ladies in charge and I think they'll be all right, but we really must find the Queen. She is deeply loved and I fear for the safety of her fairy family if she doesn't return soon.' Finished, Nib looked around for a sign. He didn't see one. 'That is all. Thank you Wizard.' Nib sat back down.

Now, before the Wizard responds to a request, three tests of worthiness must be met. First, the request must be loud enough to be heard by the Wizard wherever he happens to be in Inner Earth. Second, the requester must be a known friend of Inner Earth. And last, and most important, the request must be true.

Nib's request easily met the first two tests. In fact he yelled so loudly he startled the Wizard who was just settling down to breakfast. On his way to the table, the Wizard tripped on his pant leg, fell into his chair and sent his tea flying through the air. It landed across the room on the rug. His toast fell straight down and landed on his shoe, jam side down. The Wizard snorted at the mess.

Second, it was undisputed that Nib was a friend of Inner Earth. He had once saved an entire elfin family who failed to receive notice of one of Earth's impending earthquakes. When the Earth started to shake, the Singleton's were trapped in their Inner Earth home. Mr and Mrs Singleton cried and cried for help. Nib was nearby on the surface. He heard the crying and wished so strongly to help that a gateway appeared before him. He slipped through the gate and found the home demolished with the roof caved in. Mr Singleton called out for help. Mrs Singleton called out for her children. When she heard no response, she grew frantic. By the time Nib uncovered her, Mrs Singleton was exhausted and crying. Nib and Mr Singleton stripped away logs and debris looking for the children. Laura, Joy and John had crawled under their bed, which had collapsed on top of them. When Nib pulled the fat mattress off them they were scared, but unharmed. The mattress on top of them had muffled their cries. For a long time afterward, gifts of treats and small wooden toys appeared from time to time in Nib's mailbox. 'To Nib, from the Singletons' is all the cards said.

Following the incident, Mrs Singleton had petitioned the elfin elders and later there had been a ceremony to honor Nib. The Wizard presented Nib with a special crystal that heated up and glowed any time he was near an Inner Earth gateway. Although he was a surface elf, the glowing crystal was Nib's key to Inner Earth and he used it often. He became well known among Inner Earth elves.

The Wizard pondered the third test. Was Nib's request true? Nib's concern for the fairies seemed genuine. He had mentioned how deeply loved the Queen was. In fact, the Wizard loved her himself and he knew of the great love her fairies had for her. She was lovely in a quirky way. Her short red hair stood straight up in spikes. Her eyes were the color of the morning sky and they turned up at the corners. She appeared not to walk on the Earth, but to dance upon it. The Fairy Queen loved the Fairy Glen. Every fairy, every tree, every flower, every drop of water, and every blade of grass felt the Queen's affection. The Fairy Glen loved the Queen because she loved it. The Wizard shrunk when he imagined the great loss her disappearance must have caused. He immediately sent his intention to give directions for Nib to find the cavern.

Nib and Mc*Manigal waited in the center of Crystal Lake. Mc*Manigal had suggested a game of cards to pass the time. Gnomes were clever with cards and even though Nib knew this he chose to play. Time (like distance) was measured differently in Inner Earth. There was no way to know how long it would take for the Wizard's reply to reach them.

After his fourth loss to the beaming Mc*Manigal, Nib noticed a giant crystal glowing bright blue at the north end of the lake. It sang a clear bright note.

'That's it!' Nib's yelling woke up the cat. 'That's the way to the Wizard!'

## Chapter 3

# The Dragon World

With Iliyan clinging to his neck, StarWalker leaped toward the image of Aneurin he held in his mind. Soon, he saw a planet in the distance. It was a large world speckled purple and red in the same way Earth is speckled blue and green.

StarWalker landed in the branch of a tree. Iliyan braced herself for a fall to the ground. Instead, the tree morphed into a kind of pillow with arms that embraced them as they fell to the planet's surface. At the moment they touched down, a giant hole opened up and they fell through it. They landed softly in an underground tunnel. A moment later their entry hole sealed up.

Iliyan looked around. The tunnel was dark. Burning candles hung on the wall. The tunnel walls and floor sparkled purple and red, as if the planet was made of glitter.

'What is this place?' Iliyan asked.

'This is the East portal. I always enter here. Are you all right?'

'Yes, I've never been swallowed by a planet before.'

'Most worlds have portals to the interior. If a world looks deserted on the surface, it's likely the beings live in the interior. A portal is like a doorway and it's good if you know where they are, because they can be hard to find.'

'Do you think the Fairly Dusty Moon had beings inside?'

'Probably.'

Iliyan regarded her unlikely friend and the unusual trip they'd made. Their last leap had been onto an asteroid that was moving at great speed. They'd leaped and landed so many times, Iliyan lost count. Although the landings were abrupt, she really enjoyed the takeoffs.

'Thank you, StarWalker, that was fun.'

StarWalker swelled. He liked that Iliyan was happy with him. Dogs are always sure they are responsible for the way a person is feeling. So if you are sad, your dog feels sad too, and if you are happy, your dog is sure he is responsible. That Iliyan enjoyed the ride made StarWalker feel warm again. He looked at Iliyan. In the candlelight, her red hair appeared spun from gold. She smiled at him and he was instantly glad he'd found her.

'I can't wait for you to meet Aneurin!' StarWalker started down the hall. Iliyan stood up and walked as if she'd been walking all along. StarWalker cocked his head and looked at her. His ears flopped to one side. *Curious*, he thought. She didn't seem to have any pain. He decided not to mention it. He didn't want to remind her of one more thing she might not remember.

The farther they traveled from the East portal, the less well defined the tunnel became. The walls and floor melted together into a kind of rainbow goo. Globs of colors moved together and seemed almost liquid, but they held together just enough to be solid. Although she could clearly see him next to her, Iliyan put her hand on StarWalker's back. She'd never walked through red and purple goo before and the feeling of his fur in her hand comforted her.

*'Don't worry. Your eyes will adjust. Soon you'll be able to see,'* StarWalker comforted her.

Iliyan began to see shadows of structures in the goo. She saw extremely large doors with giant knockers on them. She saw windows and pathways, gates and fences. They were walking in a neighborhood.

A moment later a gargantuan bird towered over them. Although made of goo, and far larger than any bird she had ever seen, Iliyan recognized the shape as belonging to a crow. Just as she became aware that she'd had a memory, the bird spoke.

'Welcome, StarWalker,' it said in a soft mothering voice.

*'Hi, Elimin!'* StarWalker brushed the top of his head along the bird's wing. *'This is my friend. I found her on the Fairly Dusty Moon.'*

Elimin lowered her head. One enormous black eye stared at Iliyan. The bird's eye was larger than Iliyan's head. Elimin looked Iliyan over, up and down her front and back. Iliyan hoped she didn't look like bird food.

'Hello,' said Elimin, and she pressed the top of her head to Iliyan's chest. Iliyan hesitated then took the massive head in her hands and hugged her. The bird purred. After a moment, Elimin straightened. 'Now I will always recognize you, my dear. I have heard the song of your heart. You will always be welcome here.'

Elimin turned to StarWalker. 'Aneurin is expecting you. He came to see me a few minutes ago to tell me you were coming. Go ahead.'

Elimin stepped aside and a great gate appeared in the goo behind her. Elimin gestured with her wing and the gate opened.

'Thank you,' said Iliyan.

'See you again!' Elimin winked at Iliyan as she and StarWalker stepped through the gate and continued down the path. Iliyan noticed the outline of a figure approaching in the distance. The figure was slightly taller than she was, but it was an odd shape for sure.

StarWalker ran up to the form and danced on his hind legs in front of it. He sang a dog song. The creature sang a growling song in return. When she caught up to them, Iliyan saw a young dragon, red with black markings on his face. He was slightly taller than Iliyan. He had shining black eyes and beautiful golden tendrils that flew around his face. His teeth were shiny white.

'Hello. You must be the lost girl.' The dragon did a fancy bow similar to something one might do on stage. 'I'm Aneurin. Glad to meet you.'

'I'm glad to meet you too.' Iliyan giggled at Aneurin's formality. 'How do you know who I am? And, can you tell me anything else about myself?'

'I only know what StarWalker tells me. He can send his thoughts ahead of him. I always hear him no matter where he is. He told me he found you and that he was bringing you here.'

'*She can't remember where she's from,*' StarWalker said.

'I can't remember much of anything,' Iliyan said. 'I did recognize what kind of bird your gate guardian was, but I have no idea how I knew that.'

Aneurin and StarWalker looked at each other.

'That's odd,' said Aneurin. 'I'm glad you brought her here. She needs to see Dad.'

Aneurin turned and walked forward on the path. Iliyan rushed to keep up. She wondered if her eyes were playing tricks on her. Things appeared and disappeared in the goo. It seemed like magic. She saw a street lamp in front of her, and then it was gone. A cart appeared then disappeared. A house came into view and she forced herself not to blink. She stared at the house. A tabby cat stepped onto the stoop and eyed

StarWalker. The cat meowed. Aneurin picked up the cat and opened the door. Iliyan followed Aneurin and StarWalker inside.

Candles lit the room. It was warm and very colorful. There was a bright green couch and tables painted yellow and purple. Dragon family photographs hung on the walls. Golden colored drapes framed the view from the window, which was of the goo outside. A single step led to the sunken dining room and a large table and chairs. While the goo outside was dark and shadowy, inside everything looked bright and solid.

'Mom, we're here,' Aneurin called out. A golden dragon appeared. Her deep black eyes were the same as Aneurin's, but she was smaller. She sang to StarWalker who cooed back to her.

'Hello.' She turned to Iliyan.

'Hello.'

'I am Sulwyn, welcome to our home.'

'Thank you; I really like all the colors.'

Sulwyn guessed Iliyan wasn't from a rainbow world because her skin was an odd shade of light brown. Brown was a color not seen on rainbow worlds.

'Dragons live on rainbow worlds,' Sulwyn said. 'Those colors are the Rainbow Energy. Rainbow Energy is what dragons use to create everything.'

'You mean the goo?'

Everyone laughed. Iliyan laughed too. She was not the first visitor to the Dragon World who referred to the Rainbow Energy as 'goo.' It had a very goo-like quality.

'Well, it's very lovely to be surrounded by Rainbow Energy.' Iliyan yawned. 'It feels peaceful and calm to me. I'm a little tired.'

'You'd better get her to Dad before she falls asleep.' Rainbow Energy almost always made visitors fall asleep. It was soothing and comforting. In fact, StarWalker had already curled up in a corner of the living room on a pillow that was reserved for him. He was nearly asleep when Aneurin thumped him on the rump. 'Let's go, Bud.' StarWalker stood and shook.

'Is Dad in the lab?' Aneurin asked his mom.

'Yes, but go in the back door. He's closed for the day.' Sulwyn looked at Iliyan. 'Are you hungry?'

'No, Ma'am. I've had one of these.' Iliyan handed her sack to Sulwyn, who looked inside. She pulled out a plum and held it in her claws.

'I'll get something ready for when you're finished with Dad.' Sulwyn took the sack into the kitchen.

Aneurin, StarWalker and Iliyan walked across the street. The building in front of them had a sign with symbols on it. Iliyan had no idea what the symbols meant.

'This way!' Aneurin led them down an alley to the back of the building. The door was cracked and light spilled out. Inside, Dr Trahern was reading. The book's cover had some of the same symbols Iliyan had seen on the sign outside. Dr Trahern was immense. To say he was silver simplified the truth. From one angle he appeared violet, from another blue, still another green. He changed color as he moved.

'Hi, Dad. This is the girl StarWalker found.' Aneurin stepped out of the way. 'This is my dad. He's a doctor.'

'Hello.' The tall dragon stood. 'I am Dr Trahern. I'm pleased to meet you.'

'I'm glad to be here.' Iliyan felt drawn to him. She stepped forward and made a movement like a curtsy. She bent low and looked down at the floor. Out of the corner of her eye she noticed that her plums sat on a plate on a nearby table. She thought it odd that her plums would be there, as she had just handed them to Sulwyn a moment ago.

'Stand up child.' Dr Trahern wasn't accustomed to being bowed to and he didn't like it much.

'Come and sit down.' He pointed and walked back to his chair. Aneurin produced a chair for Iliyan and placed it opposite his dad.

'Dad, can I go to the lab?' Aneurin skipped across the room.

'Yes. You need to finish your last assignment.' Earlier, Aneurin had been working on a potion recipe. He had not had a chance to complete it before StarWalker and Iliyan arrived. StarWalker followed him to the lab on the far side of the room. Iliyan sat down in the chair opposite the doctor.

'May I see your hands?' Dr Trahern took Iliyan's hands and turned them over. Iliyan looked at the dragon's hands. Sinewy muscles stretched beneath iridescent silver scales. Long white claws positively shone. Iliyan started talking. She began at the beginning, so far as she knew. She explained that her memory began on the Fairly Dusty Moon. She mentioned her sack of plums and it was only then that she remembered she couldn't walk when StarWalker found her. She talked about leaping and landing. Although her stomach pain had disappeared when they landed on the Dragon World, she told him about it anyway. When she looked into Dr Trahern's eyes, she precisely remembered every detail of her recent journey. When she finished her tale, she was out of breath.

'May I take a look at you?' Dr Trahern asked.

'Yes, thank you.'

'Come with me.' Dr Trahern led her to a recliner where she sat comfortably. Instantly, Iliyan fell asleep. Potions exploded in the back corner.

'Aww!' Aneurin whined. He liked to make things explode. He often pretended he was practicing assignments when, in fact, he was just blowing things up. He was always sure to make a great show of disappointment when his experiments incinerated.

Dragons are telepathic and so Dr Trahern knew what Aneurin was up to. It is also true, however, that dragons love a good show (more than anyone you'll ever meet). Secretly, Dr Trahern delighted in his son's dramatics.

'Aneurin, bring me the scanner,' Dr Trahern said. Aneurin retrieved the scepter from its place on the wall. Although not large, it was heavy; so heavy he half-dragged, half-carried it across the room. Dr Trahern chuckled to himself. Every time he watched Aneurin struggle with the scepter, he remembered being a young dragon in his father's lab. He remembered how he once dropped the heavy scepter down the stairs. Helplessly, he watched it tumble end over end to the floor below, all the while wondering how he would lift it back up the stairs. It was humiliating and his memory of it was precisely the reason Dr Trahern had not put a second floor on his office.

Dr Trahern took the scepter from Aneurin. In the doctor's hands it may as well have been a baton. He tossed it from one hand to the other and removed a satchel from a drawer. Inside the satchel were crystals and other rocks. He chose from among them and inserted them into holes in the scepter. The wand nearly came to life, crystals twinkling, notes ringing. He waved it over Iliyan, scanning her as she slept. The crystals glowed in patterns and sang. Dr Trahern stopped and wrote some notes on a tablet.

'Light?' Aneurin stepped closer to see what his father was writing. 'What does that mean?'

'She is photonic, made of pure light substance.'

'What's this?' Aneurin pointed to his father's notes.

'There are traces of carbon and nitrogen in her clothes. I found the same elements in the plums Mom sent over.'

'What does that mean?'

'It means she likely comes from a carbon world.' Dr Trahern changed the crystals in the scanner and turned back to Iliyan. This time parts of her body lit up as he waved the scepter over her. Aneurin saw what looked like a purple rock around Iliyan's heart and something else, dark maroon, in the center of her head.

'What's that?'

'I'm not sure.' Dr Trahern scratched his head with one gleaming nail then pointed at Iliyan's head. 'This maroon mass in her head may explain why she can't remember anything; the purple mass in her heart may explain why she doesn't seem terribly concerned about her lack of memory. The mass is blocking her heart from feeling anything too intensely. It may be protecting her. Let's work on the head mass and see what happens. We should protect her heart in case her memories are very traumatic. This way she will remain protected until she knows more about herself.'

Dr Trahern set down the scepter. He whispered a few words in ancient dragon and gently blew a fine stream of fire out his nostrils onto Iliyan's forehead. The fire was a rainbow. It surrounded Iliyan's head, but it did not burn her. Aneurin watched as the fire penetrated her skin. The maroon mass began to break up. Dr Trahern continued to blow. He toned a note. Once broken up, the mass disappeared. Dr Trahern changed his tone and continued to blow. Silver fire engulfed Iliyan's head until it positively sparkled. When he was done, he spoke more words in ancient dragon. Then, he scanned her body again. The purple mass remained in her heart, but her head was clear.

'What's that?' Aneurin pointed to a silver grid-like structure that materialized above Iliyan's head.

Dr Trahern and Aneurin watched as the structure grew up from Iliyan's head. Finely spun platinum waves of light rose up from Iliyan's forehead in increasingly wider circles. Among the waves of gleaming light, bright crystals and other stones appeared that twinkled pink, turquoise and lavender. The dragons looked at each other. Sitting on the top of Iliyan's head was a gleaming crown.

'She's a queen!' Aneurin squeaked and he ran to wake up StarWalker. 'You have to see this, Bud,' he said as he shook his friend awake.

They all stared at Iliyan. The crown had grown up seven layers. Each layer had a particular crystal or stone. As Iliyan awoke the stones twinkled brighter. She saw the doctor and her friends staring at her.

'I'm Iliyan,' she blurted.

Dr Trahern handed her a mirror from a large collection of gadgets that sat beside him.

'I'm a queen? Yes! I'm a Fairy Queen.' Iliyan smiled broadly into the mirror. A moment later she panicked. 'Oh no! The Fairy Glen!'

'*What's a Fairy Glen?*' StarWalker asked.

'That's where I live. And I take care of all the fairies there. They need me. I'm sure they're very upset. I have to get home.'

'Where is home?' Aneurin asked.

'Gaia.' Iliyan said.

'Gaia?' the three sang in unison. Aneurin and Dr Trahern looked at each other. They scanned their memories for anything they might know about Iliyan's home. They knew of fairy worlds, but not one of them had heard of Gaia.

'What can you tell us about Gaia, dear?' Dr Trahern asked her.

'She is beautiful. She is green and blue. There is a sun that rises and sets, so that the sky is blue in the day and black at night, with stars. The Fairy Glen is a grassy meadow that sits between a forest and a lake. The lake is full of clear blue water that feeds the plants. We have flowers in all colors. We have rainbows, but only in the sky. There is no goo. We fairies take care of all the growing things.'

'Is it a surface world then?' Dr Trahern asked.

'Well, yes. And no. There are elves and other elementals that live in the interior. The Wizard lives in the interior. The rest of us live on the surface with human beings.'

'Human beings?' Dr Trahern furrowed his brow.

'Yes.'

'And you live among them?'

'No. They live in houses. When they come to the Glen, we hide. It's easy. Only some of the small ones can see us.'

Iliyan went on for some time in a rather encyclopedic fashion, reciting facts about Gaia. Dr Trahern, Aneurin and StarWalker watched and listened with great interest.

'May I have some water?' Instantly, a glass of water appeared in her hand. The collective eyebrows of Dr Trahern, Aneurin and StarWalker rose.

'Fairies can do that.' Iliyan gulped the water. 'If I think of something I want, it appears in front of me.'

This was the first time StarWalker or the dragons had seen anything like that. Dragons make things out of Rainbow Energy by imagining a needed thing that then takes shape or molds itself from the goo. It takes a moment or two and the taking shape is something you can watch. Once a thing is in form it separates from the goo and at that point it appears on its own in space. It doesn't take long, but it is a gradual process. Iliyan's glass of water had appeared instantly. She drank the water and refilled the glass. When she was done, the glass disappeared. She noticed her friends staring at her.

'Oh, we can make things disappear too.'

'Disappear, indeed!' Dr Trahern snorted. 'Perhaps that is a clue as to why you are here.' He told her about the purple mass in her head and how he had cleared it.

'I can remember everything now. Thank you.'

'You're most welcome, but we are not finished. When I scanned you, I noticed a similar mass in your chest, near your heart.' He took the scepter and held it in front of Iliyan's heart. The red mass glowed.

'What is that?' Iliyan touched her chest.

'I'm not sure. Whatever it is, it is impairing the normal functioning of that area. The mass in your head most definitely weakened your memory. I suspect this mass is altering your ability to know how you feel. Removing it will likely cause you to have clear recollection of your feelings, in the same way that removing the mass in your head made it possible for you to clearly remember facts. You will feel everything you have ever felt; every sadness, every happiness, everything. I need your permission to go ahead and remove it.'

'Yes. Please.'

'Very well then.' Dr Trahern opened his pouch and chose some crystals. He replaced the crystals on the scepter. He spoke ancient dragon again and breathed the rainbow colored fire onto Iliyan's chest. The scepter twinkled and sang. Aneurin and StarWalker watched as the mass in Iliyan's chest moved and changed shape. It became smaller. The doctor toned a note. Once the mass had broken up, Dr Trahern breathed silver fire on Iliyan's chest to seal the area. He asked Iliyan to sing a note. The note she chose was identical to the one he'd chosen to seal the area in her head.

When he was finished he used the scepter to scan Iliyan's body. Her body twinkled and shone under the crystal scepter.

'That should do it.' Dr Trahern returned the crystals to the satchel. Iliyan started to cry. StarWalker put his head in her lap.

'I have to get home. I still don't remember how I got here.'

As she sat crying, Dr Trahern noticed another sparkling grid-like structure forming behind Iliyan's shoulders. He nudged Aneurin and pointed to Iliyan's back. StarWalker noticed it too. Iliyan was pushed out of the chair as two fully-formed gossamer wings grew out of the center of her back. Their edges glowed lavender and green and their tips extended from her ears to her knees. She flapped them slowly together and apart. Stars dripped from the tips and fell to the floor. They glowed a moment, popped, and then disappeared. Iliyan stood in the center of an explosion of tiny stars.

# Chapter 4

# The Wizard's Cavern

Nib rowed toward the glowing singing crystal. It seemed a long while before the boat made any progress. Finally, the crystal grew slowly larger as Nib rowed. At its base, the crystal was the size of a small mountain. Its blue glow illuminated half the lake. He looked around the base of the giant crystal, but he didn't see the Wizard.

'Great!' Nib was tired of riddles. 'What do we do now?'

'Maybe there's a clue on the shore.' Mc*Manigal was tired, too.

'Yes! Right. Maybe.' Nib rowed along the crystal's base looking for a clue. The longer he rowed the shorter his patience became. He was just about to yell out something to the Wizard when he heard a splash in the water behind him.

'Over there!' Mc*Manigal yelled, pointing back toward the center of the lake. Nib turned the boat and rowed. When they arrived at what seemed the location of the splash, Nib and Mc*Manigal looked first at each other, then they stared at the lake. They waited. The lake was calm and quiet. Eventually another splash occurred behind them. They whirled around in the boat, nearly capsizing it, and barely caught sight of the back half of a flying fish.

'There!' Mc*Manigal pointed. Again Nib turned the boat around and rowed. They arrived in the location of the splashing, and waited. As Nib stood staring, a loud growl startled him so that he nearly jumped head first into the water. The cat sat up, annoyed.

'My stomach.' Mc*Manigal looked embarrassed. 'I wish we'd brought some food.'

'Me too.' Nib regretted not thinking to pack food. He scanned the water and waited.

Although no one can say for sure exactly how long Nib and Mc*Manigal pursued the flying fish, one can say that the adventurers went on in this manner for some time: splash, point, row, wait... splash, point, row, wait.... Finally, feeling he was the butt end of a joke, Nib erupted in frustration.

'Wizard! That is enough!'

As a rule, elves are fond of mirth and mischief, but Nib was weary from battling the rapids and rowing in circles. He was anxious to arrive at his destination.

Nib rowed the boat back to the crystal's base. He rowed along, wondering what to do next. He rowed around a corner and saw a rivulet that flowed between two giant crystals.

'I didn't see that before. Maybe that's it!' Nib turned the boat into the rivulet. He heard the massive crystal go silent behind him. He thanked the blue crystal and he felt the rock's reply in the water's vibration beneath him. The rivulet was calm and peaceful. When a cave came into view in the distance, the cat moved to the front of the boat. He looked at Nib and meowed what, unmistakably, was a cat order. Nib turned into the cave and, for a while, he rowed in utter darkness. He didn't want to run aground, but he kept rowing anyway.

Presently, a light ahead revealed the cave was a tunnel. Everyone squinted as they passed out of the dark tunnel into bright light. Nib stopped the boat.

'I don't believe I've ever seen anything like this,' Mc*Manigal said as they rowed into a great large cavern. Brightly lit singing crystals of all imaginable colors lined its walls and ceiling. This was a magnificent place indeed.

'Well, which way now?' Nib said to the cat. The cat looked out into the distance and Nib rowed in the direction he looked. As they approached the water's edge at the far end of the cavern, Nib saw a castle rise up out of the crystals. It appeared to be made of frosting. The turrets looked like red licorice, the walls like stacks of marshmallows.

'It's a candy castle,' Nib said.

'We should be so lucky.' Mc*Manigal's stomach growled again. He jumped out of the boat and pulled it onto shore. Nib turned back to thank the cat, but he was gone.

'Funny, I didn't see where the cat went.'

Mc*Manigal didn't reply. He was happy the cat was gone.

Nib and Mc*Manigal walked toward the castle gate. It was locked. Nib banged on the gate. Nothing happened.

'Do you think the Wizard lives here?' Mc*Manigal asked as they pressed their faces to the bars and surveyed the castle grounds.

'I'm sure of it,' said Nib.

Mc*Manigal felt something touch the back of his neck. He tried to swipe it away. Instead, his hand brushed against it. It was fuzzy. He turned around.

'Uh, Nib. You might want to see this.' Mc*Manigal's voice quivered.

'Yea, what is it?' Nib said, his face still pressed to the bars of the gate.

'Uh...,' was all Mc*Manigal could manage. Nib turned and froze. The eight eyes of an enormous green spider looked at them.

'We are here to see the Wizard,' Nib squeaked.

'Is he expecting you?' the spider said in a little girl's voice.

'Yes, I believe he is.'

'Who are you?'

'I am Nib, and this is Mc*Manigal. We need the Wizard's help.'

'What seems to be the trouble? Maybe I can help. I have many talents.'

'Do you have anything to eat?' Mc*Manigal asked.

'Just flies. Oh, and jelly beans.'

'Jelly beans are my favorite,' Mc*Manigal said. 'Do you have any green ones?' The spider ambled away and returned with a basket full of green jelly beans.

'Thank you!' Mc*Manigal said, his mouth full of beans. 'What is your name?'

'Lucy,' said the spider.

'Well, Lucy, you have made my stomach very pleased indeed.'

'You're quite welcome.'

'Who made this castle?' Nib asked.

'The Wizard mostly, but we all help out where we can,' said Lucy.

'My silk makes hammocks and curtains. Also if I spin in a pile, it makes a nice pillow. Get on my back. I'll take you to the castle. It's farther away than it looks.'

Just a few moments before, Mc*Manigal would never have mounted the back of an enormous spider. With his mouth full, he took one long leap and landed in the center of Lucy's back.

'Well, come on, Nib. What are you waiting for? The lady said, "Get on!"' Green spit flew out of Mc*Manigal's mouth. Nib laughed and climbed up Lucy's back. The gate opened by itself and Lucy ambled through it. Nib had never ridden a spider. He'd never met a spider that insisted on it. It was a very smooth ride. The spider's eight legs operated so that there were at least two legs on each side touching the ground at all times. They traveled up the path to the castle. For a long time, the castle didn't get any closer. In fact, once or twice Nib looked away, and when he looked back, he could have sworn the castle appeared farther away. Mc*Manigal whistled a tune when his mouth wasn't full of jelly beans. When Lucy arrived at the steps to the castle entrance, the doors opened and she walked up the steps and across the threshold into an enormous circular entrance hall. She continued across the hall and up the grand staircase. At the top of the stairs, she turned and walked along the second floor railing back toward the front of the castle. She stopped at a door.

'This is the library. You'll find the Wizard inside,' she said. Mc*Manigal and Nib hopped off.

'Thanks Lucy,' Nib said. Mc*Manigal tipped his hat.

'My pleasure. We don't get many visitors here, and never ones as charming as you.' Lucy winked four of her eight eyes at Mc*Manigal. He turned a curious shade of purple. Nib laughed.

'I think she was flirting with you,' Nib said after Lucy crawled away.

'Don't be ridiculous.' Mc*Manigal turned away so Nib couldn't see him blush.

Inside the library were shelves of books that went upwards forever. There were two ladders on either side of the room that one could roll along the face of the shelves. Nib and Mc*Manigal looked around. There was a great wooden desk in the center of the room. Several hammocks hung from posts.

'Hello.' Nib's voice echoed.

'Merau,' was the reply. The black cat sat on a table near the window.

'There you are.' Nib walked over to the cat and scratched his ears until he purred. 'You must have taken a short cut.'

'I see you've met Binxley,' boomed a voice from the top of one of the ladders. Nib looked up.

'Hello Wizard,' Nib called up the ladder. 'Yes, he traveled with us all the way here.'

'He wanted to make sure you made it here before lunch,' said the Wizard. 'He gets cranky when lunch is delayed.' The Wizard climbed down the ladder.

'Is it time for lunch then?' Mc*Manigal asked.

'Indeed it is,' said the Wizard as he reached the library floor. He slapped Nib on the back. Mc*Manigal extended his hand for a shake. The Wizard pumped his hand vigorously. Several ornate platinum rings shone in the light that streamed in from the window. The Wizard's bright eyes gleamed black. His long white beard hung halfway to his belly. He was nearly twice as tall as the gnome, but not as tall as Nib. His purple pointed hat flopped to one side and golden ribbons adorned its brim. His purple velvet jacket hung to his knees and covered his tattered brown trousers. His wide smile flashed a glittering golden tooth.

'I'm Mc*Manigal,' the gnome said.

'Yes, I know,' said the Wizard. 'Please, come this way.'

The Wizard gathered Binxley in his arms and pushed his way through a side door. Nib and Mc*Manigal followed. The door opened to a dining room with a very long table. Windows lined the front wall. The view of the crystal cavern dominated the room. The table was set, two seats at one end and two seats at the other. Nib looked at Mc*Manigal.

'You two sit here,' the Wizard said as he walked past the near end of the table. The Wizard continued across the room and sat at the other end of the table. Binxley sat on a stool beside him.

'I don't mean to be inhospitable, but Binxley and I don't talk much when we eat. We like to concentrate. Just wish for whatever it is you'd like to eat.'

Nib was full of questions, but he knew this was not the time to ask them. He looked at his plate and thought of his mother's vegetable stew and cornbread. He blinked his eyes and his lunch appeared. He enjoyed it without speaking. Mc*Manigal chose mushrooms and turnips on a bed of greens. Light streamed in the window as if it were a sunny day. (In fact, there is no sun in Inner Earth. The light comes from the crystals.) Nib wondered if the crystals ever slept, or if the cavern was brightly lit all the time. He hoped to remember to ask the Wizard that question, when questions were allowed.

When the Wizard finished eating, he set down his napkin and pushed away from the table. He picked up Binxley and walked toward Nib and Mc*Manigal.

'Nap time,' he yawned and pushed the door to the library open. Nib and Mc*Manigal followed him. The Wizard climbed into a hammock and stretched out. Binxley turned three circles in the center of the Wizard's chest and settled down to preen. Nib and Mc*Manigal stood looking at one another.

'Forgive me,' said the Wizard. 'Choose any hammock you like.' He waved his hand in a circle.

Nib and Mc*Manigal climbed into hammocks. Mc*Manigal wondered if Lucy had spun the one he chose. It was very soft and comfortable and before long he was snoring. Nib looked around the library. He'd never seen so many books. He wondered if the Wizard had read them all. He looked out the window as sleep closed in on him. He saw the light from the crystal cavern dim as though it were suddenly dusk. In the next moment, he was asleep.

Nib dreamed he was at home in the Elfin Village with his friends. They were playing tag and he heard his mother's voice call him. He turned to see where she was. He saw a dog. The dog was white with floppy ears and a tail that curled high over his back. The dog appeared to sing, as there were notes coming from his moving mouth. Nib looked past the dog for his mother. He did not see her. Although he was dreaming, Nib was aware that he thought his mother must have been looking for him. He had left in such a hurry he had not told her where he was going. He hoped she didn't worry. The dog sang again. This time it made an unpleasant scraping sound that woke him up.

Mc*Manigal dragged a chair across the library floor. He climbed up to a stack of books and studied the titles. A moment later he took one from the shelf and sat in the chair. His feet dangled off the edge.

'What's that?' Nib asked.

'It's about celestial navigation. You know, navigating by the stars. Not much use in Inner Earth, but it might come in handy the next time my brother and I go fishing.'

'Where do you fish?'

'Mostly on the Crescent River. I wish I'd had my pole back there at the Crystal Lake. I could have had the last laugh on that flying fish.'

'Maybe.' Nib snorted when he laughed. 'Have you seen the Wizard?'

'Nope. He was gone when I woke up. The cat's gone too.'

Just then the library door opened. The Wizard, books piled high in his arms, held the door open for Binxley.

'Go on then, I haven't all day,' said the Wizard. Binxley swished into the room. The Wizard spilled the books onto the desk. 'Good. You're up,' he said. 'You slept well, yes?'

'Very well,' said Mc*Manigal.

'Nib?'

'Yes, sir. I feel much better, thanks.'

'Good. We have work to do. Now, did either of you have any dreams?'

'I had one just as I was waking up,' said Nib.

'Excellent,' said the Wizard. 'Those dreams are always some type of message artfully placed by yourself near the end of your sleep so you'll remember them. What was it?'

'It was a dog,' said Nib. 'He was all white with long floppy ears and a bushy curling tail, and he sort of sang these deep notes. I thought I heard my mother call me, but I didn't see her anywhere.'

'A singing dog.' The Wizard stroked his beard. 'Curious.'

'Wizard, how am I going to find the Fairy Queen?' Nib asked.

'An excellent question.' The Wizard pushed the books around on his desk. 'I don't know. I've been looking into fairy magic, hoping to find an answer. Tell me what you know about Iliyan's disappearance.'

Nib told the Wizard about the state of the Fairy Glen and that both the Queen and her brother, Prince Kelm, had been missing for two days.

'They disappeared without a trace.'

'Do the fairies have any idea where they may have gone?'

'Not that I found out.'

'Do they suspect foul play?'

'Nobody knows. Nobody saw or heard anything. Of course they suspect foul play. So long as their plants are alive, fairies don't leave them. The Fairy Queen has never left the Glen before.'

'Who benefits from the Queen's disappearance?'

'Well, I put Eritha in charge, but it came as a surprise to her. I think the only reason she accepted was she knew the Fairy Glen wouldn't survive long with Iliyan gone.'

'So you don't think it was a power grab?' the Wizard asked.

'I don't think so,' said Nib. Nib couldn't imagine fairies grasping for power. Nib didn't know whether power was important to fairies. The Wizard's questions were wise and designed to rule out possible reasons the Queen might have disappeared. They made Nib think.

'Curious,' the Wizard said. 'I think we need to consult Wallace.'

'Who's Wallace?' Nib asked.

'That's my crystal ball.' The Wizard walked to the window and removed a scarf that covered a round object in the center of a table. The Wizard sat down, pulling his chair in very close to the table. He stared into the ball and he motioned for Nib to sit opposite him at the table.

'Look carefully at Wallace, Nib. Tell me if you see anything.' The Wizard addressed the sparkling globe, 'Wallace, we're looking for the Fairy Queen. Her name is Iliyan. She's been missing two days.' To Nib he said, 'Do we know what she was wearing when she left?'

'A dress and red boots,' Nib said without taking his eyes off the ball. Wallace turned a cloudy violet. Black lightning struck, then dozens of stars appeared.

'Tell him Prince Kelm is gone too,' said Nib.

'Tell him yourself,' the Wizard snapped. 'He's not deaf.'

'Wallace, the Queen's brother, Prince Kelm, is missing too.'

Wallace turned a shade of dark red, became darker still, then suddenly cleared.

'I see a snow-covered mountaintop,' said Nib.

'Yes,' said the Wizard.

'Where is it?' Nib asked the ball.

'Just wait a moment,' said the Wizard. 'Show us more, Wallace.'

The crystal ball orbited the mountain. Nib and the Wizard watched as Wallace showed them all sides of it. Oddly, one side of the tip of the mountain's peak had no snow on it at all. From that side, the peak resembled a silver needle that pierced through a cloud of snow.

'Stop,' said the Wizard as the silver snowless peak came into view. 'That needle could be ice.'

'Wallace, can you show us where the Prince is?' Nib asked.

The crystal ball orbited again around the mountain's peak, then moved across the Earth's surface. Finally, a single picture was visible. It was a beautiful tree-lined meadow in spring. The snow-covered mountain with the silver pointed peak was in the background.

'That's beautiful,' Nib said.

'Wallace, does this place have a name?' the Wizard asked.

Wallace's picture cleared and a word appeared.

'Heaven.'

'Heaven?' The Wizard shook his head. 'It looks like Earth to me. I've seen mountains on Earth that look like that.'

'Does this mean the Prince is dead?' Nib asked.

'I don't know,' said the Wizard.

'Do you have an atlas?' Nib asked.

'Geography is at the top of the far ladder, on the shelf to the left.' The Wizard covered Wallace with the scarf.

Nib climbed the ladder. At the top he found a number of books of maps. He chose the largest *World Atlas* on the shelf. Nib struggled down the ladder while clutching the giant volume under his arm. He dropped the atlas on the desk and opened its cover.

'What are you looking for?' Mc*Manigal looked up from *Celestial Navigation*.

'Mountains,' said Nib. In a chapter on Earth's mountains, Nib found a list of the highest ones. He looked at the list: Mount Everest, K2, Kanchenjunga, Lhotse I, Makalu I, Cho Oyu, Dhaulagiri, Manaslu I, Nanga Parbat, and Annapurna I. All but one was in the Himalayas.

The Wizard looked through the largest book in the room. It was mounted on its own table near the desk.

'What book is that?' Nib asked.

'It is the *Unabridged Nature Being Dictionary*, with human references. I'm looking up 'heaven'. There is a long entry here. For humans, heaven is a beautiful place they go when they die.'

'Is it located on Earth?' Nib asked.

'No. Earth exists in the third dimension. Human heaven is not. So no, it isn't on Earth,' said the Wizard.

'Hmm' said Nib and he returned to the *World Atlas*. He looked up each of the mountains on the list. 'Listen to this. The ninth highest mountain on Earth is called Nanga Parbat. It is in the Western Himalayas. It has the tallest mountain face on Earth, called the Rupal Face, which rises 15,000 feet above the mountain's base. The face is nearly vertical. No snow can fall there. It is covered with ice sheets. Here's a picture.' Nib pushed the *Atlas* across the table to the Wizard and pointed at the page. 'Look, no snow on the top. Do you have a book on the Himalayas?'

'Up with the maps somewhere.' The Wizard motioned to the ladder without looking up from the *Atlas*.

'Hey Mac,' Nib called to Mc*Manigal, 'would you go up and look for a book on the Himalayas?'

'Who are you calling Mac?' Mc*Manigal asked. 'You want me to go all the way up there.' The gnome pointed and looked through his eyebrows. 'You don't know much about gnomes, do you? We like our feet on the ground. Sorry.'

'Never mind.' Nib pushed his chair back from the desk and started up the ladder. As he climbed, the Wizard returned to the *Unabridged Nature Being Dictionary*.

'Here's something,' said the Wizard. 'Fairy heaven refers to a place called Fairy Meadows.' Nib listened from the top of the ladder. He pulled himself along the railing and the great ladder rolled back and forth in front of the shelves. He was getting pretty good at hanging off the ladder while pulling books off the shelf and putting them back. Finally, he found a book called *The Himalayas*. He looked in the book while hanging onto the ladder.

'Is Fairy Meadows on Earth?' Nib asked.

'Yes, in Kashmir.'

'Where's that?' asked Mc*Manigal.

'Look it up,' said the Wizard and he pointed to the Atlas.

Nib tucked *The Himalayas* under his arm and started down the ladder. More confident this time, he took the stairs three and four rungs at a time. He practically flew all the way down.

Nib joined Mc*Manigal and the Wizard at the desk. He checked the index in *The Himalayas* for Nanga Parbat and turned to its page. Nib saw a picture identical to the one Crystal Wallace had shown them.

'Here it is!' Nib said. Mc*Manigal and the Wizard moved closer.

'It looks cold there,' said Mc*Manigal.

'It's almost twenty-seven thousand feet up,' said Nib. 'Hey! This picture was taken from Fairy Meadows.'

'Fairy heaven,' said the Wizard. They looked at each other.

'That's it!' Nib said.

'Indeed,' said the Wizard.

'That's what?' Mc*Manigal was confused.

'That's where Prince Kelm is,' said Nib.

'According to a rock,' said Mc*Manigal. Nib shot Mc*Manigal a dirty look.

'It's the only clue I have,' Nib said. 'Wizard, how do I get there? Do I really have to hike up twenty-seven thousand feet? And how do I get the Prince back from there? I mean, he's a fairy. He flew there, why can't he fly himself home?' The more Nib grasped the difficulty of the situation, the faster he talked. He had more questions than answers.

'Hold on there, Nib. You forget. I am a Wizard.'

'Okay, so can you use a scepter or something?'

'My scepter is good for changing the form of things. It's not the tool for transporting someone who may not want to be transported. For that, one of us will have to go.'

'Is there an easy way to get there?'

'Easy? No. Quick? Perhaps.'

'Quick is good,' Nib said, feeling encouraged and anxious. 'How do we do that?'

'You can exit Inner Earth through the portal that runs between the Indian and Eurasian tectonic plates. That's the closest portal to the Himalayas. Then you have to locate Nanga Parbat and find Fairy Meadows.' The Wizard gathered maps and a compass. He put the items in a shoulder bag along with some crystals. He held up a bright green crystal. 'This one will help you find food and water,' he said.

Nib felt sick. He sat down and put his head in his hands. He was thinking this was a big mistake. The Wizard knelt in front of him.

'Nib, this is not as difficult as you think. You can do this. You would not have accepted this quest if you were not able to meet its challenges.'

'Sure! That's what you tell everybody,' Nib said without looking up.

'That's right. I do.' The Wizard sat next to Nib. 'Every quest seeker has felt as you do right now. In any worthwhile adventure there are points at which the quest appears impossible, but that is an illusion and a test of your persistence. If it were true that quests are impossible, no one would ever complete one. Do you want to find Iliyan?'

'I have to. I promised Kopo and his family. I can't give up and still return to the Fairy Glen.'

'That's it then,' said the Wizard. 'Simple. You can't go home. You can't stay here. Binxley doesn't like houseguests. You're going to Kashmir.' The Wizard handed him the shoulder bag.

'Okay, but I still don't see how,' Nib sighed.

'You're going to ride on Fiona,' the Wizard said.

'Who is Fiona?'

'She's a golden eagle. Come!' The Wizard led Nib out the door of the library. Nib followed him three or four steps down the hall before he realized Mc*Manigal was not behind them. He turned back and opened the door to the library. Mc*Manigal stood in the center of the room, rooted into the floor, a panicked look on his face. Nib looked at him.

'Come on, Mac! We gotta go!'

'I can't ride on an eagle, Nib. I can't go twenty-seven thousand feet up. I can't go ten feet up. I've never even climbed a tree!'

'You heard what the Wizard said, Mac. You wouldn't have accepted this quest if you didn't have what it takes to complete it. Besides, you can't stay here. Binxley doesn't like you.'

Mc*Manigal looked at the cat. Binxley hunched his back. His butt shook. The tip of his tail rattled a cat warning. Mc*Manigal ran for the door.

## Chapter 5

# The Fairy Star

Dr Trahern closed the door to his office and followed Aneurin, StarWalker and Iliyan across the road to the house. Inside, the dining room table overflowed with plum-colored food. Sulwyn carried serving dishes from the kitchen.

'Please sit down,' she said. 'Dinner is ready.'

Aneurin bounded over to his mother and took the dishes from her. He didn't recognize the food. 'What is this, Mom?'

'You'll see,' Sulwyn winked at her son. 'Go tell your sister it's dinner time.'

Aneurin turned toward the stairs. StarWalker followed Sulwyn back into the kitchen.

'Isabel!' Aneurin shouted up the stairs. 'Dinner's ready!'

In the kitchen, StarWalker transmitted a telepathic image to Sulwyn. It was a picture of the cheese he'd enjoyed earlier that day. Sulwyn was an excellent food artist. She could create any kind of delicious food.

'Cheese?' Sulwyn asked.

'Yes,' said StarWalker. *'It was creamy and delicious.'*

'Okay, I'll see what I can whip up for you. Go sit down.' Sulwyn patted the dog's head.

Iliyan came through the kitchen door as StarWalker went back into the dining room. 'Can I help?' Iliyan asked. Sulwyn looked at her crown and wings.

'My, my,' she said. 'You are very lovely. How do you feel?'

'Strange,' said Iliyan. She sat heavily upon a stool at the counter. 'I feel better knowing who I am and where I come from, but I feel terrible about my friends on Gaia. I know they are worried.' Sulwyn hugged Iliyan tightly. Iliyan could feel the mother dragon's heartbeat.

There is something wonderful that happens when one is in the company of dragons. One feels utterly welcome and at home. Iliyan felt this. Although the fate of the Fairy Glen and how to get back loomed heavy on her mind, she was among family. Iliyan didn't remember her mother and father. The fairies in the Glen were the only family she knew. This feeling of being home in a strange place felt odd, and she liked it. She was glad to be on the Dragon World.

'I am so grateful to be here,' Iliyan said. 'I'm so glad StarWalker found me.'

'So are we, dear,' Sulwyn said. 'Now don't worry. One cannot solve problems if one is lost in worry. StarWalker and Aneurin are very good at finding lost things. You are in good hands. Help me take these things to the table.' Iliyan and Sulwyn carried the rest of the food to the dining room.

Isabel came down the stairs. She was a lavender dragon, shorter than her brother. She liked to hug. At the bottom of the stairs she hugged StarWalker and he sang to her. She sang him a dragon tune. When she saw Iliyan she stopped. 'Wow! You're a fairy! I've never actually seen a fairy before. I've read books where dragons and fairies are friends. You're pretty,' Isabel gushed, and hugged Iliyan.

'Thank you,' said Iliyan. 'So are you.'

Isabel blushed deep maroon.

'Everyone please sit down,' Dr Trahern boomed. At that they all sat.

'What's this?' Aneurin asked as he picked up a serving dish.

'Plum pudding.' Sulwyn pointed to a plum-colored mountain in a bright yellow bowl. 'And this is mashed plums with plum jam. This is a plum pie and this is plum pasta with plum sauce.' Sulwyn pointed to purple noodles with a darker purple sauce.

'You made all this for me?' Iliyan asked.

'Not at all, dear,' Sulwyn said. 'I was inspired by your plums, that's all.'

'Do dragons eat plums?'

'They do today. Dig in!' Sulwyn handed Dr Trahern a serving spoon. Everyone ate. The plum dishes were delicious.

'Thanks Mom, this is great!' Isabel said. 'Iliyan, what else do fairies eat?'

'We eat what grows in the Glen on Gaia. Nuts and berries are our favorites.'

'What's a glen?' asked Isabel.

Iliyan told Isabel about Gaia and the Fairy Glen.

'Are there dragons on Gaia?' asked Isabel.

'I've never seen one.'

'Is the Rainbow Energy there?'

'No. The colors are blue and green mostly. The beings are tan-colored, like me,' said Iliyan.

'If there's no Rainbow Energy, what do humans use to make things?' Aneurin asked.

'They use Gaia,' said Iliyan. 'They use trees and parts of plants. Fairies cry when humans cut down trees. We think they must not know that trees are alive. We worry about the trees, and all the black stuff.'

'What black stuff?' Aneurin scooped extra sauce on his mashed plums.

'Humans pour hot, sticky, black stuff on Gaia's surface. When it cools, it hardens so humans can wheel their vehicles on it, but it chokes the planet. It kills the plants and nothing grows where it is. More and more, this black stuff covers the surface. We fairies think the humans must not know Gaia is alive either.'

'Can't you tell them?' Isabel dished up a slice of plum pie.

'We try, but they can't see us or hear us.'

'Why not?' Isabel couldn't imagine not being able to see Iliyan, who was sitting right next to her.

'Fairies have learned to hide from humans. For a long time we tried to be among them, but instead of making friends, we scared them. So we chose to hide. We live at a frequency that is just beyond what humans can see. This way we can go about our business and not scare them.'

'I can't believe none of them can see you, you're so real.' Isabel pinched Iliyan.

'Ouch!' Iliyan giggled and tickled Isabel. 'Some of the children can see us. It's very surprising when they do. We've been hidden for so long. We fly right up to them and play with their hair, and still they don't see us. So it comes as a shock when a little human walks into the Glen and talks to us. We have made friends with them. We make stories with them. They build us little fairy houses out of sticks and leaves, and put flowers in them. We love the little houses.

'How are we going to find Gaia?' Sulwyn asked. The table hushed. Everyone looked at everyone else.

'I have an idea,' said Aneurin. 'We could visit the Fairy Star. It isn't Gaia, but there are fairies there and they may know something.'

'Fairies! In space?' Iliyan laughed.

'Yes,' said Aneurin. 'They look like you except they are different colors. Some of them are very small like the Gaia fairies you describe. I've visited there several times. I have friends there.'

'How do we get there?' Iliyan asked.

'I have to prepare an orb for us to travel in. The Fairy Star isn't so much in a place as it is in a space. The orb will allow us to travel through the dimensions of space until we find it.'

'Fairies use orbs on Earth,' said Iliyan. 'Humans can't see orbs either.'

'Are humans dangerous?' Isabel asked.

'I've never met one who was,' said Iliyan. 'But they are easily frightened, and once frightened it's hard to know what they will do. They can be destructive and messy. Sometimes I hear Gaia groan under the weight of all the things humans build. I don't think they understand how heavy they are.'

'Fairies must work very hard.' Sulwyn stacked plates.

'We do. Our Glen is very beautiful. The lake is clean enough for fairies to swim in. I have seen dogs swim in the lake too.'

*'Dogs!'* StarWalker looked up. *'Like me?'*

'None as beautiful as you.' Iliyan rubbed his ears.

*'I shall like to see these dogs. Is there cheese on Gaia?'*

'Yes. It is a favorite food of humans, dogs, and elves.' Iliyan took StarWalker's face in her hands and kissed the end of his nose.

*'Let's go!'* StarWalker jumped up.

Aneurin laughed. 'You said the magic word Iliyan. If there is cheese, StarWalker will find it. Thanks, Mom. Dinner was great.' He stood up and kissed the top of his mother's head. 'Are you guys ready?'

*'For cheese! You bet!'* StarWalker said.

'Do you want these?' Sulwyn held out Iliyan's sack of plums.

'Please keep them.' Iliyan marveled at how the plums had traveled to Dr Trahern's office and back, had been turned into many delicious dishes, and never left the paper sack. 'Thank you for everything.' *Dragons are magical*, she thought. She hugged Isabel and whispered to her, 'I hope to see you again.'

'You are most welcome anytime. Good luck to you,' said Dr Trahern.

'Come on! Get in!' Aneurin had blown a silver-white bubble in the living room. They stepped inside. A rainbow formed around the outside of the orb. Lights swirled all around. From inside the orb, only the rainbow was visible.

'Everyone think of the Fairy Star,' said Aneurin. 'Think hard.'

'I've never been there,' said Iliyan.

'It doesn't matter. Just imagine fairies.' Aneurin closed his eyes. Iliyan

*Alyson Budde*

could not help imagining the Fairy Glen and her fairy family on Gaia. She saw her brother, Prince Kelm, and her cousins Eritha and Lauren. She imagined them dancing. StarWalker did not remember the Fairy Star. Iliyan was the only fairy he knew, so he thought about her. After a few moments, StarWalker saw a plant appear outside the orb. Then he saw another. The plants seemed to multiply until all around the orb was a lush garden. He nudged Aneurin with his nose.

Aneurin opened his eyes. 'This is it!'

Iliyan opened her eyes. Aneurin breathed on the orb and it popped and disappeared. They stood in the center of a garden. Iliyan looked around at all the plants and flowers. She didn't recognize any of them, although they looked similar to the ones on Gaia. Some of the plants towered far over her head and their flowers were many times her size.

'What now?' Iliyan asked.

'I'm not sure. Let's look around.' Aneurin approached the tallest plant. It was the size of a very old tree, and it had droopy, yellow, teacup-shaped flowers that were nearly the size of Aneurin. He flew up to take a closer look. He could see his reflection in the flowers' shiny black stamens. He flew from flower to flower looking at himself.

Iliyan approached a vine that wound around itself. She followed its sinewy branches in and out of each other. It was like playing a game to see where each vine branch ended and she enjoyed herself. Every now and again she thought she heard an odd high-pitched giggle. Iliyan knew this was the sound of a fairy. 'Come out, come out, wherever you are!' Iliyan sang, remembering how much her fairies liked to sing and play hiding games.

StarWalker followed his nose. He found the smelliest plant in the garden. It had long, spiked, silver leaves that grew straight up. At the end of the leaves were bell-shaped purple flowers. StarWalker sniffed at one of the stinky flowers and sneezed a very big sneeze. The flower shook at the force of StarWalker's sneeze and out of its center popped the tiniest of fairies. He was yellow. He had red feathers for hair, red and white striped socks, a green overcoat and a purple cap. A vine was slung over his shoulder. His wings beat quickly. He flew over and landed on StarWalker's nose. StarWalker looked cross-eyed at the little fairy. When Aneurin caught up to him, StarWalker had nearly fallen over from staring at the fairy on the end of his nose.

'Who do we have here?' Aneurin asked as the fairy flew up to look Aneurin in the eye.

StarWalker shook the dizziness off. *'I don't know. I sneezed him out of the stink plant.'*

Aneurin looked at the little fairy, who jumped onto his nose. Now, Aneurin went cross-eyed too.

Iliyan emerged from the vine maze. She saw StarWalker and Aneurin teetering a little. Then she spotted the little fairy. 'Oh! Look at you!' She flew over. The little fairy flew up to Iliyan's face. He flew all around her crown. Iliyan put out her hand and he landed in her palm.

'You're pretty,' said the little fairy.

'So are you,' said Iliyan. 'What is your name?'

'I am Mister Tim.'

'I am Iliyan and these are my friends, StarWalker and Aneurin.'

'Where did you come from?'

'We came from the Dragon World,' said Iliyan.

'We're looking for a planet called Gaia,' said Aneurin. 'There are fairies who live there.'

'It is my home.' Iliyan could see from Mister Tim's expression that he didn't know anything about Gaia. 'Is there anyone here who might know about Gaia?'

'If there is anything to know, King Luran would know it.' Mister Tim took off. 'Follow me! I can take you to him.' Although small, Mister Tim flew quickly. Iliyan flew along behind him. Aneurin took flight to keep up and StarWalker jogged along. They wound their way through the garden until they came to a vine-covered path.

'What is this place?' Iliyan asked.

'This is the Hall of Flowers,' said Mister Tim. 'The walls are made of every different kind of flower, all of them in bloom.' The floor was carpeted with fallen flower petals that StarWalker kicked up as he ran through them. The smell was heavenly. Iliyan floated along. At the end of the Hall of Flowers were two enormous red doors.

'What's this?' Aneurin asked.

'These are the Council Chambers.' Mister Tim waved a small wand and began a spell to open the doors.

'Council?' Iliyan interrupted.

'The Council of Twelve,' said Mister Tim. 'They are the fairies who are in charge. Rather, the Council and King Luran. He's probably inside.'

'Am I to meet the King?' Iliyan asked.

'Yes.' Mister Tim straightened his hat. 'He must know you are here.'

'Is there a certain way I am supposed to greet him?' Iliyan felt nervous. She wasn't sure she was ready to meet the King.

'You can flutter your wings if you want to.' Mister Tim winked at StarWalker. 'But you don't have to. We are not very formal.' Iliyan fussed with her dress.

*Just be yourself,* StarWalker said.

'Very well.' Iliyan sighed. 'I am ready.'

'Iklog! Taminum lorwine paruti esala!' Mister Tim commanded with a wave of his wand. Stars dripped from the tip of his wand and the two massive doors opened inward together. Iliyan heard a conversation stop abruptly. Mister Tim flew through the open doors. StarWalker and Aneurin stood behind Iliyan, who didn't move.

*'It's okay,'* StarWalker said telepathically. *'We're here.'*

Iliyan looked back and motioned for her friends to move up and stand beside her. They moved into positions at her right and left hands. She looked at both of them. Together they walked into the Council Chambers.

Inside the Council Chambers, the Council of Twelve sat along the edge of a great stone ring. The stone was pink quartz with sparkles in it. In its center sat another pink quartz stone shaped like a pointed mushroom. King Luran, dressed in a maroon coat and wearing a simple gold crown, sat at the ring directly opposite the doors. Once clear of the doors, Iliyan stood still with Aneurin and StarWalker beside her. Mister Tim flew across the room and fluttered at King Luran's ear. Iliyan could barely make out Mister Tim's faint explanation. When Mister Tim finished, King Luran rose.

'Welcome visitors.' He walked around the ring to greet Iliyan, who nervously fluttered her wings.

'Good King Luran, I am Iliyan, Fairy Queen from Gaia. These are my friends: Aneurin, from the Dragon World, and StarWalker,' she hesitated, 'from space.'

'We are pleased to see you. Thank you for coming directly here.' King Luran reached out his hands for Iliyan. She reached forward. He held her hands in his and stared at them, turning them over. He looked at her face for a long moment as if studying her. Iliyan thought she saw tears form in his eyes. She felt a great love travel through her body. She looked at the King. Behind him a chair appeared that had not been there the moment before.

'Please sit down.' He motioned toward the chair. Aneurin and StarWalker sat on the floor on either side of Iliyan.

The Council of Twelve had remained silent. They were all fairies of varying sizes and colors. There were men and women and a few children. Some had crowns.

'What can we do for you?' King Luran asked.

'Sir, I am looking for my home, Gaia. I appeared mysteriously in space and I do not know how to get back. My friends brought me here. We hoped you might be able to help.'

For a moment, no one said anything. King Luran stood listening as though someone was speaking. He turned toward the Council and nodded. 'Thank you,' he said.

Iliyan understood the Council had conferred about her in such a way that she could not hear them. King Luran walked back around the Council ring and sat down in his chair.

'What can you tell us about Gaia, Iliyan?' he asked.

'Well sir, it is not a fairy world like this. It is a human world.'

'Do you live among the humans then?'

'Oh no. We did once, but now fairies stay hidden. We live in the natural places.'

'Why do you stay hidden?'

'Humans don't believe fairies are real. Seeing us scares them. We don't like to scare them.'

'Is this true of all humans?'

'All except some children.'

King Luran leaned forward, more interested. 'The children can see you?'

'Yes, some can. More and more they come to the Fairy Glen and dance in the fairy ring. We love to play with them. They bring us candy and build houses for us. They treat us with love and friendship.'

'And what of the planet?'

'She is beautiful. We love her like a mother and we work very hard to take care of her. Still, we feel as if there is more we should be doing, but we don't know what that is. Sometimes I hear Gaia moaning.'

'What is her burden?' King Luran asked.

'Humans things,' said Iliyan. 'Humans are builders. They build structures and vehicles. They don't fly so they require many different kinds of transport vehicles. Some of the vehicles carry many, many humans. They look heavy to me.'

'Do the humans take care of Gaia?'

'I'm not sure they know how to,' said Iliyan. 'They're very good builders, but they're messy. There's a lot of trash. We encourage them to pick up the trash. The little ones help us with this.'

King Luran and the Council of Twelve looked at each other. They held a silent, private conversation for some time. Iliyan looked at Aneurin and StarWalker. She put her hand on the dog's head.

Finally, the King spoke. 'I'm sorry Iliyan, I cannot tell you where Gaia is, but I do have something that may help you locate your home. Please follow me.' He walked to the red doors. Iliyan rose and curtsied to the Council of Twelve, and then she turned and followed King Luran out of the chamber and into the hall. StarWalker and Aneurin loped along behind her. They walked down some stairs and through an endless labyrinth of halls with closed doors. King Luran stopped before a set of doors with symbols on them. He waved his hands in front of him and closed his eyes.

'MA he shay ah toly nee ca doley ah mo nee a. Zhan zahn coo la me apoola she vavee day ze oh. Plea deli na koo avee a,' he said. The doors opened. King Luran moved into the pitch-black room. Once inside, he toned a note. Slowly the room glowed turquoise from the light of a single crystal. Iliyan could see crystals of all sizes and shapes lining the walls of the room. It was a crystal museum.

King Luran walked through and stopped before a pink crystal that sat on a dark red, velvet pillow. It was five-sided with a single silver speck inside it that shone like a star. Four sides of the crystal were rough. The fifth side was perfectly smooth. King Luran handed the stone to Iliyan. It fit in her hand. When she closed her hand around it she felt its energy rush through her body. She heard it beg her not to put it down. The stone felt like a very close friend and Iliyan felt compelled to protect it. She held it tight in her hand. StarWalker and Aneurin noticed that Iliyan's crown glowed brighter with the crystal in her hand.

'It seems like I know this stone,' she said.

'And it knows you,' said the King.

'How is that possible?'

'Is it possible you've been here before?' King Luran asked.

Iliyan started to say, 'No.' Then she remembered how quickly and completely she had forgotten Gaia when she found herself on the Fairly Dusty Moon. 'I don't remember being here before, but I suppose it is possible,' she said. 'I've had some problems with forgetting.'

'This stone is for you. Perhaps it will help you remember,' the King said.

Iliyan's hand caressed the stone. 'Thank you, I will take good care of it.'

'There is another stone I need to give to you,' said King Luran. 'It is large.' They walked through the room and stopped in front of a beautiful green stone.

'This is the Capstone Crystal. It must go with you,' said the King. 'There is a Dying Star somewhere in the universe that needs this stone. You must find the star and deposit this stone deep in its core. The results of this task will aid you in your search for Gaia.'

'How will we find the star?' Iliyan asked.

'One of you has been there before,' said King Luran. Iliyan and StarWalker looked at each other, then they both looked at Aneurin. They shrugged in unison.

'Oh, this is hopeless,' said Iliyan. 'Only one of us can remember anything. Aneurin, does this make any sense to you?' Aneurin walked closer to the stone and looked at it for a long moment.

'If you touch it, it will speak to you,' said King Luran.

Aneurin grasped the stone in his hands, his claws barely stretching around the fat stone. He looked at it and waited. He felt the energy of the stone travel through his claws and up his arms, flooding his body. As it traveled into his head, Aneurin had a vision of a very bright star. He saw the other stars around it and noted their pattern.

'I don't remember being there, but I can see it. I will know it if we find it.' Aneurin hoped he'd been convincing enough. He picked up the stone and hovered in the room. Mister Tim appeared.

'Take Iliyan and her friends back to the gate,' King Luran instructed Mister Tim. King Luran then reached for Iliyan's hands. 'Thank you for coming. I wish we could be more help to you at this time. I feel you will find your way back. Gaia needs you. Perhaps there is a larger reason for all of this.' He kissed each hand once and held them to his face for a moment. He kissed the pink crystal. 'Goodbye,' he whispered. Iliyan was sure she saw a tear in his eye.

'Good luck to you all,' he said, then he winked at Iliyan and he disappeared.

Iliyan felt her heart leap. She wished she could follow him. 'Thank you,' she called out to the space where he had been.

'This way,' said Mister Tim and he flew back in the direction of the door. Iliyan hesitated. She looked at the pink crystal and at the space where the King had stood. Holding the pink crystal tightly in her hand, she followed StarWalker, Aneurin and Mister Tim into the hall. Mister Tim repeated the invocation the King had spoken. The doors to the crystal museum closed. Mister Tim turned and flew down the hallway. Iliyan and Aneurin took flight and StarWalker ran to keep up. Iliyan looked forward to flying down the long labyrinthine hall. Her feelings were all mixed up and she imagined the distraction of flying through a maze would make her feel better. She was still looking for the labyrinth when the hallway suddenly dissolved into the garden. Immediately, they all stopped in front of Mister Tim's stinky plant. The travelers looked at each other, clearly startled at how quickly they'd arrived back in the garden.

'Short cut!' Mister Tim giggled.

Several small fairies brought vines. They took the Capstone Crystal from Aneurin and fastened it to his chest. Once in place, Aneurin could hardly feel its size or weight.

'Thanks.' Aneurin checked the vines. The fairies squeaked, then disappeared.

'I think we'll fly home,' Aneurin said to Iliyan and StarWalker. 'The orb is great, but you can't always see clearly outside of it. If we fly, we'll be able to see everything. Maybe we can find the Dying Star. Are you ready?'

'*Ready!*' StarWalker sang.

'Let's go!' Aneurin yelled with wings in full flap. StarWalker crouched and sprang into space. Iliyan looked back at the garden. Some small part of her did not want to leave. She wanted to remember King Luran and the Fairy Star. She stood, soaking up as much of the feeling of the Fairy Star as she could. She held the small crystal close to her heart. She felt love from the crystal filling her heart. When she felt full, she took flight. As she flew away, the beautiful pink Fairy Star glowed bright and twinkled behind her.

# Chapter 6

# Prince Kelm

'Are you ready, Mac?' Nib tucked the shoulder bag between his feet.

'Always ready.' Mc*Manigal looked cross as he settled himself in the second seat of the eagle's elaborate leather saddle.

Nib waved to the Wizard.

'Now remember,' the Wizard called to Nib, 'if you want to go in a particular direction, you must look there. Focus is your only navigation tool and the way you communicate with Fiona. She will go where you look, so stay focused.'

'Yes sir!' Nib was anxious to get started.

The Wizard looked at Mc*Manigal. 'As the navigator, you should be looking all around you at all times. Fiona won't run into anything, but you may see something that you want to tell Nib about. You can communicate with him using a system of numbers. Imagine that your field of view is like a circle around your head. Use the image of a clock to give directions. If something is directly in front of you, it is at twelve o'clock. If something is behind you, it is at six o'clock. Is that clear?'

'So you would be at three o'clock.' Mc*Manigal looked at the Wizard who was on the ground to his right.

'Precisely!' said the Wizard. 'Stay safe boys.'

'Let's go!' Nib said and he focused his eyes on the sky straight up and ahead of them. He felt his body lean in that direction. The leaning wasn't necessary, but it felt good to have something more to do. The saddle shifted slightly as Fiona took off. Mc*Manigal's stomach leaped into his throat. He grabbed the saddle with both hands and hoped he didn't throw up.

Fiona flew through Inner Earth. She navigated passages that appeared too small for her to fit through, by pressing her wings close to her body. She flew through dark tunnels and along a river. She passed a crashing waterfall. Mc*Manigal watched the water plunge into the river below. Soon, a bright light appeared in the distance. As they approached the light, Nib saw it was an opening to Surface Earth. He focused on the light and Fiona flew directly for it. She flew across the threshold onto Surface Earth. Bright daylight flashed. Mc*Manigal shielded his eyes with his hands. Nib squinted but kept his focus.

Mc*Manigal repeated a mantra. It went: *'Don't look down. Whatever you do, don't look down!'* Now, it is a strongly disciplined person who follows his own advice. Willing one's self not to look at something, or not to think of something, or not to eat the last cookie in the jar, or not to search for the hidden birthday presents, never works. One focuses one's attention completely on the thing one is supposed not to do. In fact, willing one's self not to do a thing practically guarantees the doing of it. Poor Mc*Manigal. If only he had a distraction. For instance, a lovely slice of pie would take his mind off the increasing distance between him and the ground. But, there was no pie here. He could not deny that he was in a saddle, mounted on an eagle, flying through space, and he could not stop himself from looking down.

When Mc*Manigal looked down his stomach overtook him. He

didn't know whether he was going to pass out or throw up, or both. When he finally pulled his gaze up from the ground, he felt better. He noticed the view. He remembered the Wizard had told him to look around. The vast amount of space around him hypnotized him and he felt better.

As a rule, gnomes are earth-bound. They like to feel earth beneath their feet. As children, gnomes are not tree climbers or swimmers. They are not fond of heights. Mc*Manigal knew he was seeing something very few gnomes ever saw: Earth from the air. He knew from the Wizard's library that the Himalayan Mountains included some of the tallest mountain peaks on Earth. Mc*Manigal marveled at the long stretches of pure white peaks that rolled before him as far as he could see. It made him feel better when he reminded himself that those peaks were Earth.

Nib flew Fiona up and over the top of a snow-capped peak. Forests and other small patches of green sprinkled the ground. Nib searched for Nanga Parbat. All the while he kept his focus in order to fly Fiona; he also kept a picture of Nanga Parbat's snowless, pointed peak in his mind.

Before long, Nib felt strongly that he had forgotten something. At his feet sat the shoulder bag the Wizard had given them. He couldn't remember any other thing he might have needed. He thought about Mc*Manigal, but he was sure he hadn't forgotten his friend. His certainty that he'd forgotten something grew stronger and stronger. Finally, unable to ignore the urge, Nib turned Fiona around.

'Whoa!' Mc*Manigal yelled. 'Hold on there, Sparky!'

Nib yelled over his shoulder. 'I'm afraid I've forgotten something. I'm turning back.'

'Take it easy and don't lose your focus.'

Fiona turned without disturbing her riders and headed back in the direction from which she'd come. Nib and Mc*Manigal saw the backsides of the peaks they'd passed. Nib looked at them closely. One of the peaks was snowless and pointed.

'There!' Nib steered Fiona straight for the peak. It looked like Nanga Parbat's nearly vertical Rupal Face. Nib could see the face was covered with ice.

'The Rupal Face!' Nib yelled.

'Humph,' grunted Mc*Manigal. 'Are we there yet?'

'Almost,' said Nib. He knew from his research that the Rupal Face was east facing. Fairy Meadows was south of Nanga Parbat. Nib steered Fiona up over the snowless peak and turned slightly left. He flew her closer to the ground.

Nib called back to Mc*Manigal. 'Look for the meadow!'

'You check nine and I'll check three.' Mc*Manigal used directions the Wizard had suggested.

'I can't check nine. I have to watch where we're going,' Nib said.

'Right, Chief. Never mind.' Mc*Manigal scanned the horizon. He was excited and he was glad to have a job. The sooner Fiona landed the better.

'There it is!' Mc*Manigal pointed so violently the saddle nearly shifted.

'Where?' Nib struggled not to shift his gaze.

'Two o'clock.' The Wizard's navigation suggestion had worked. Nib knew exactly where to look. On the ground, at exactly what would be the two o'clock position on a clock, Nib saw a green meadow and forest.

He focused on the meadow beneath them. Fiona circled and landed. Mc*Manigal scrambled out of the saddle and down the tail of the bird. He grabbed the ropes to steady himself as he went.

'Do we tie her up?' he asked.

'I don't think she's going anywhere, but it's probably a good idea just the same. I'd hate to be stuck here.' Nib climbed down and tied one of Fiona's ropes to a tree. Then he spoke to the bird.

'Thank you. That was a great trip.' He stroked her as Fiona rubbed her head against Nib's shoulder. 'Now we're going to go into that forest. We won't be long. You wait here.' Nib took a drink from his water flask and offered it to Mc*Manigal.

'Not yet, thanks.' Mc*Manigal held his stomach. 'I'm still queasy.'

'Let's go!' Nib looked around the meadow. He knew fairies didn't just come out and greet visitors. They must be coaxed from their hiding places. In the Fairy Glen at home he flushed out fairies by playing hide and seek. He knew the fairies there and he would tease them by name. He didn't think hide and seek would work in Fairy Meadows. Fairies love music, dancing and games. Nib was a terrible dancer so he pulled out his panpipes and blew a tune as they entered the forest. As they walked, Nib remembered his arrows game. He removed his neckerchief and prepared it as a blindfold. He selected a tree in the nearby forest.

'Stay behind me, Mac,' he whispered to Mc*Manigal. A bird screeched a loud call somewhere overhead. Fiona screeched her response. Nib fastened his blindfold and drew an arrow from his quiver. He pulled the arrow back on his bow and shot. Fling, then thud. The arrow flew to the tree and pierced the bark. Without removing his blindfold, Nib drew and shot two more arrows. He did not hear those arrows strike anything. He pulled off his blindfold. He looked back at Mc*Manigal while he reset his bow on his shoulder and ran into the forest. Mc*Manigal jaunted along. Nib pulled his arrow from the tree. He ran his hand over the wound in the bark. 'Thank you,' he said.

'Bull's eye, with a blindfold on! That's impressive, Nib.' Mc*Manigal examined the bark where the arrow had pierced it. The bark healed itself while Mc*Manigal looked at it. Mc*Manigal examined the perfect bark. 'I wouldn't have believed it unless I'd seen it myself.'

'I can only hit one out of three.' Nib searched the forest floor near the tree. 'The hard part is finding the ones that don't hit. They could be anywhere.' Nib put his hand on Mc*Manigal's arm to get the gnomes attention. Then, with the first two fingers of his right hand, Nib pointed to his own two eyes, and then he pointed out into the forest. Mc*Manigal understood the signal to mean he should look around. He walked into the forest, kicking over leaves and sticks as he went.

'Sometimes fairies help me find my arrows,' Nib said loudly in a singsong voice.

'I've had good help from fairies myself,' Mc*Manigal played along. All the while they kept a look out for sharp flashes of light and color in their peripheral vision that might indicate the nearness of fairies. Nib's two arrows were nowhere to be found. Neither was Prince Kelm, or any other fairy for that matter.

'Surely there must be fairies in Fairy Meadows.' Nib kicked the dirt. He and Mc*Manigal walked on until dusk. Nib played his panpipes, but they saw nothing. As night rolled into the meadow, Nib's mood soured. He tried to hide his disappointment, but he was crabby. He wanted to yell out a demand that the fairies appear, but he knew one could not go around ordering fairies to appear and expect to be successful. He decided to wait until morning and try his game again. Two arrows had disappeared. Surely the fairies had taken them. Perhaps they could be enticed into taking some more. Mc*Manigal could be positioned in the forest to watch. It would be dangerous, but Nib could tear holes in his blindfold so he didn't shoot his friend.

'We should head back and set up camp.'

Nib turned to leave the forest. Just then, a blue light flashed at the corner of his eye. He whirled back around. 'Aha! I caught you!' he said. Nothing moved. Nib kicked the ground. 'Aww! I saw you,' Nib whined. Frustrated and out of ideas, Nib jumped in half circles and whooped and hollered in a playful way, hoping to flush out a fairy. Silence. Mc*Manigal thought Nib looked like a lunatic. Nib clearly was willing to try anything. Mc*Manigal thought about how anxious he was to get back to his own forest. He decided if jumping and hollering would complete this mission, he was not above that. Mc*Manigal started jumping and hollering. The two of them jumped and hollered until they wore themselves out.

'No fair,' Nib panted. 'I saw you.' He stood up and straightened his quiver. 'Let's go, Mac.' They walked out of the forest. Nib walked to Fiona and rubbed her chest. She purred. He unfastened the basket she carried between her legs. A tent, bedrolls and a lantern were packed inside the basket. Nib climbed up to the saddle and retrieved the shoulder bag. He took out the food and split it into four portions. He gave a portion to Mc*Manigal and took one for himself. He had decided if they hadn't found Prince Kelm in two days' time, they would give up.

Mc*Manigal chewed on crusty bread and a small piece of cheese. He and Nib shared an apple for dessert. It was just enough food to keep their stomachs from grumbling in the night. After they ate, Mc*Manigal pitched the tent.

Nib rested near the tent and considered their predicament. That his arrows had disappeared seemed a good sign. Someone must have taken them. Fairies were good at making things disappear, however, they couldn't always bring them back. That Nib was a stranger in Fairy Meadows was a handicap. Fairies were shy. He wondered how to overcome this disadvantage. Nib had seen Prince Kelm once or twice, but they were not acquainted. He didn't expect Prince Kelm to recognize him.

As the sun set, Nib looked around the meadow. In the Wizard's library Nib had read that human explorers had named the meadow 'Fairy Meadows' because it was so beautiful. They imagined it must be fairy heaven; the place fairies went to die. Nib thought the idea strange. He had never known a fairy who died. He wasn't even sure they did.

Nib sat outside the tent long after the half-moon rose in the sky. He listened to Mc*Manigal snoring in the tent. Finally, he blew out the lantern and slipped into the tent. He crawled into his sleeping bag and zipped it up. He closed his eyes. Against the back of his closed eyelids he saw Prince Kelm's face. Nib opened his eyes. The face disappeared. He closed his eyes again and there was Prince Kelm's face again.

'I'm looking for you.' Nib stared at the face.

'Why?' the face asked.

'Because you're missing.'

'I'm here,' said Prince Kelm.

'Where's Iliyan?'

'I don't know.'

'You're both missing,' said Nib.

'I know.'

'You know?' Nib was unable to hide his irritation. 'Then why are you here?'

'You wouldn't understand.'

'Try me,' Nib snorted. There was no response. 'We have to find Iliyan.'

'I can't help with that,' said Prince Kelm.

Nib sat bolt upright up in the tent. He opened his eyes. Prince Kelm's face disappeared, but Nib kept talking, out loud now, his voice growing angry.

'What do you mean you can't help with that? Halfway around the world there is a glen full of fairies in danger of extinction because of your disappearance. They are your fairies and all you can say is you "can't help with that." I think you can help with that!'

'Sorry,' Prince Kelm's voice said.

'Sorry!' Nib was on his feet now, pacing outside the tent. 'What do you mean? I came all this way to find you. I volunteered! Because your fairies needed help! Mc*Manigal volunteered and he's afraid of heights! And all you can say is "Sorry!" Well, that's not going to cut it. You have to help.'

'It's my fault she's gone.' Prince Kelm's voice was so quiet that Nib almost didn't hear it.

'What?' He squinted into the darkness trying to see the Prince.

'You heard me,' said the voice.

'What did you do?' Nib sounded like his mother.

'I'm not sure. I was practicing a magic trick and I made her disappear. I tried, but I couldn't bring her back.' As he spoke, Prince Kelm materialized in front of Nib.

Kelm was a Fay fairy, twice as tall as Nib. He had short brown wavy hair that hung in his face. He wore brown trousers and a yellow vest with shiny gold buttons. His wings were folded and, from one end to the other, they were nearly as tall as he was.

'How did you end up here?' Nib sat cross-legged on the ground.

'I don't know. I felt terrible about Iliyan, but I didn't know what to do. I just appeared here.'

'Did you say any other magic spells?'

'No. I wished I was dead.'

'You wished that? Are you crazy? Wishes are magic.'

'Well, it didn't work.' Prince Kelm turned away from Nib. 'I just ended up here.'

'Yes, in Fairy Meadows. Named by humans because they thought it was so beautiful it must be where fairies go to die. You're in fairy heaven.'

'But I'm not dead.'

'Thank goodness!' Nib threw his hands up in the air. 'Look, you've got to snap out of it and come with us.'

'I already told you I can't find her,' Prince Kelm snapped at Nib.

Nib stared at the fairy prince. 'You're wrong! You're the only one who can find her. We have to go. Now!'

Mc*Manigal had awakened and was listening from inside the tent. He pushed open the tent flaps. 'Fancy meeting you here.'

'Help me pack up,' Nib barked. 'We're leaving.'

Prince Kelm helped Mc*Manigal roll up the tent and sleeping bags. Nib gathered the supplies. Together they strapped everything to Fiona's belly. Mc*Manigal climbed up into his saddle, dreading the flight home. Nib climbed up after him. Prince Kelm was the last in the line.

'Sit here.' Nib squished himself to the side of his seat. The Prince climbed in the saddle. Nib held out his open hand. 'My arrows disappeared.'

'Yes,' said Prince Kelm.

'I want them back?'

Prince Kelm looked down. 'I don't know where they are.'

Nib sighed.

*Pathetic,* thought Mc*Manigal. *Bad magic, indeed.* Prince Kelm couldn't even bring back a couple of arrows. How was he going to find Iliyan?

'Okay, we can fix this.' Nib refocused on Fiona. 'Hang on.' Fiona took off more gracefully this time. She followed Nib's focus precisely. Mc*Manigal didn't feel sick. Nib was worked up, but he was grateful to have something go right.

On the way to the Inner Earth gate, Nib's mind raced with questions. *Why wasn't Iliyan with Prince Kelm? Where was she? How did Prince Kelm end up on the other side of the Earth? Was it magic? If he wished he were dead, why was he still alive?*

'Do fairies die?' Nib wondered out loud.

'I've never known a fairy who died.'

'I didn't know fairies practiced magic.'

'Fairies don't practice magic. Fairies play with light energy. We wish for what we want and the light makes it appear. That's co-creation. There's no magic in that.'

'How did you get involved in magic?'

'I was bored. My sister is the Fairy Queen. She has a job. The little fairies come to her for help all day long. She's busy. I don't really have a job. I started playing with magic because I didn't have anything else to do.'

Nib didn't understand being bored. Nib didn't really have a job, but he did what came up. There was always plenty to do.

'I've never been bored.'

'You're lucky.'

'I just do what comes up.'

'Is your sister a Queen?'

'No.' Nib didn't have any sisters. He tried to imagine having a sister, or a brother who was very important. He couldn't form a very clear picture in his mind, but what he could see made him feel small. He wondered if Prince Kelm felt small.

The three travelers ducked as Fiona flew through the Inner Earth gate. The gate wasn't narrow, but it felt that way. One moment they flew in the vast expanse of the Himalayas, and the next moment they were enclosed in Inner Earth.

Fiona flew down lighted tunnels deep into the Earth. When she came to a large clearing, she circled and landed. Mc*Manigal leaped off the bird, delighted his air travel days were behind him. Nib followed Prince Kelm down Fiona's tail.

'Now what?' Prince Kelm looked around.

Nib spotted Binxley lying on the ground in a small patch of bright sunlight. 'Hi Binxley,' he said. 'Are you waiting for us?' Binxley stretched and rolled back and forth in his personal sun patch. Nib walked over and scratched his ears. Binxley pressed his head against Nib's hand.

'A friend of yours?' Prince Kelm asked.

'A friend of the Wizard,' Nib corrected him. 'Binx, did you come to show us the way to the Wizard?'

'Merau.' Binxley stood up. The patch of bright sunlight disappeared as the cat walked off. The others followed close behind. At the edge of a clearing the cat entered a dark tunnel.

'Mac, how about you go first.' Nib hesitated. 'We need your eyes.'

Mc*Manigal moved to the head of the line. Gnomes never see complete darkness. Even the blackest night appears illuminated, as if by the light of a full moon. In the tunnel, Nib and Prince Kelm saw only pitch black.

'How about you whistle a little tune so we know where you are,' said Nib. 'I wouldn't want to step on you.'

Mc*Manigal ignored what seemed like an underestimation of his abilities. (As if he would allow himself to be stepped on by an elf and a fairy.) Still, he whistled a tune. He enjoyed whistling and the tunnel provided a pleasing echo. The whistling made it possible for Nib and Prince Kelm to move through the tunnel without falling over each other. The rhythm passed the time. Soon they heard tones coming from the

Earth. Nib knew the cavern was near. At the end of the tunnel they walked into the Wizard's cavern.

'Wow!' The sight of the brightly lit crystal cavern made Prince Kelm gasp. His whole body tingled from the colors and the sound. The tones changed as they walked into the cavern. It was as if the presence of the travelers had caused the crystals to change their tones. Mc*Manigal saw Lucy.

'Welcome back, handsome.' Lucy winked all eight eyes at the same time.

'Hello!' Mc*Manigal hurried toward Lucy, hoping she had a snack to share.

'Would you like some jelly beans?'

'I was hoping you would ask that.'

'I've just picked a fresh batch. My basket is by the gate.' Lucy noticed Prince Kelm. 'Who are you?'

'I am Kelm, Fairy Prince from Surface Earth.' Kelm bowed.

'Lovely to meet you,' said Lucy. 'I am Lucy, Gatekeeper to the Wizard. Hop on!' Nib followed Kelm up the Spider's back. Mc*Manigal grabbed the basket and climbed up behind them. Lucy opened the gate and walked up the path to the castle. The trees in front of the castle looked like cotton candy stuck on Popsicle sticks. The bushes looked like the trees, without the sticks. Lucy went through the open front doors. This time she did not climb the stairs. She turned right and walked down the hall. She stopped at the hall's end. 'You'll find him in there.' Lucy pointed with three of her legs.

'Thank you Lucy!' Nib hopped off. 'Good to see you again.'

'You're welcome,' Lucy said over her shoulder as she trotted off down the hall and out the main doors.

Mc*Manigal looked down and saw he still held Lucy's basket. 'Wait! Your basket!'

'Keep it!' she said over her shoulder. 'I'll spin another.'

Nib opened the door to the Wizard's laboratory. The Wizard stood on a stool at a counter facing the door. He blew bubbles into a tube. The bubbles traveled down the tube until they fell into a clear pot. When the pot was full, the Wizard waved his wand. There was a 'pop' sound and a rainbow shot out of the pot and flew through the air toward Nib. Nib thought it would fly right out the door, but it stopped above him and circled his head twice. Nib heard another 'pop' and the rainbow disappeared.

Nib looked back at the Wizard just before he staggered a few steps, then fell over. The rainbow had made him dizzy.

The Wizard roared with laughter. 'That's what too much Rainbow Energy will do!' He scrambled off the stool and walked over to help Nib up.

'Wow!' Nib shook his head to clear it. 'Rainbow Energy can really go to your head.'

The Wizard sniggered. 'Welcome back, boys!'

Mc*Manigal's stomach growled.

'Merau,' said Binxley, who sat at the end of the lab table.

'What's that Binx? Lunchtime? Excellent!' The Wizard gathered the cat. Binxley buried his head in the Wizard's hand. The cat's purr could be heard across the room.

'Wizard, this is Prince Kelm,' said Nib.

'Yes, yes, sorry.' The Wizard extended his hand. 'Binxley told me you were on your way. Top job, Nib. I knew you could find him. Pleased to meet you Kelm. Come along.'

'I'm glad to be here.' Prince Kelm shook the Wizard's hand.

The Wizard opened the side door of the lab. The travelers entered a dining room that looked identical to the one Nib and Mc*Manigal had been in before. Nib thought hard. He was sure the dining room they'd eaten in before had been on the second floor, next to the library. When he walked into the room, he recognized the view as being the one from the second floor dining room. Nib turned around a couple of times.

The Wizard stood watching him. 'Are you finished?'

Nib looked confused. 'It's just…' Nib stammered.

'Never mind,' said the Wizard. 'You think too much.'

This time, there were three place settings at the near end of the table. Nib sat at the table's end and motioned for Mc*Manigal and Kelm to sit on either side of him. The Wizard took Binxley to the other end of the long table. He put the cat on the table and sat down. Immediately a plate of live anchovies appeared in front of the cat.

'Ugh.' Mc*Manigal was grateful for the table's length. He imagined acorns, mushrooms and crusty bread. When they appeared, he ate without speaking. Nib ate cheese and crusty bread. Kelm had berries.

After lunch the Wizard led the procession out of the dining room. They walked back through the door from which they had entered. They should have been back in the lab, except the lab had disappeared. Instead, they were in the library. Nib laughed. He enjoyed magic.

'Nap time boys,' the Wizard announced as he prepared to climb into his hammock. Nib and Mc*Manigal did the same.

'Excuse me, Sir,' said Prince Kelm.

'He speaks! Yes, your majesty?' The Wizard giggled. Nib and Mc*Manigal giggled, too. 'I've always wanted to say that,' the Wizard said and he climbed into his hammock.

'With all due respect Wizard, shouldn't we be searching for Iliyan?' Prince Kelm asked. 'After all, time is fleeting.'

The Wizard sat up straight. 'It is? How do you know that?'

'It's just that it's been days since my sister disappeared.'

'Days?'

'In Surface Earth time.'

'Oh, so she's lost on the surface then?' the Wizard chided.

'Well I don't know. I thought since I was lost on the surface...'

'You were lost?' The Wizard's teasing continued. Nib considered rescuing the Prince from the Wizard's mounting ire, but he was entertained by the exchange. He was glad he wasn't in the hot seat.

'Did you not wish yourself to Fairy Meadows?' The Wizard waited for a response that didn't come. 'Dear Prince, there is much you may never know about magic, but I'm surprised at how much you have forgotten about being a fairy. Time is relative, and opportunities present themselves when they are least expected, and nap time is sacred.'

'Fairies don't nap,' Prince Kelm snipped at the Wizard.

'Perhaps that is the reason fairy magic fails.' The Wizard punched his pillow into place and closed his eyes. 'Pleasant dreams,' he said and he settled his hat over his face. Binxley jumped on his chest and began his daily grooming. The light in the room faded.

# Chapter 7

# Gaia's Wish

Iliyan sighed a melancholy tone. She stretched out on Aneurin's bed and StarWalker curled up on the floor beside her. In the last moments before they left the Fairy Star, she felt she was leaving something important behind. She felt she'd remembered leaving the star once before. *How can I remember leaving a place I've never been?* A strong desire to stay there had nagged her ever since. *I can't stay there. What about the Fairy Glen?* In this way she argued with herself for some time. She finally decided that even though her feelings did not make sense, she could not deny she felt them. Mister Tim and King Luran were the first fairies she had met who weren't from Gaia. How very like her they seemed. She sighed again. StarWalker looked up at her.

'Are you okay?'

'Just a bit dizzy from traveling.' Iliyan played with StarWalker's ear. 'I feel like I've been to the Fairy Star before, but I can't remember precisely. I just feel in my heart that I belong there.'

StarWalker didn't understand what Iliyan meant when she said she felt she belonged on the Fairy Star. Although he was comfortable in Aneurin's home with the dragon family, StarWalker knew it was a dragon world and he was a dog. He wondered if there was a dog world, and if he found such a world, would he want to stay there? He thought about Gaia.

Even though it was a human world, Iliyan said there were dogs there. StarWalker had spent his life leaping through space. He so loved leaping. He sighed. Iliyan hugged him. He really liked it when she did.

'It's okay.' She hung off the edge of the bed and held StarWalker's face in her hands. She flopped his ears back and forth. 'Everything will be okay.'

StarWalker's ears went up. He'd heard a squeak. Iliyan's hands were close to his ears. In one hand she held the pink crystal King Luran had given her. StarWalker nudged the hand that held the crystal. Iliyan opened her hand. The crystal vibrated in her hand as if it were alive. Iliyan held the stone up to her face. She gazed at the star inside. It twinkled.

'Twinkle, twinkle little star,' she gazed into it, 'how I wonder what you are.' The star twinkled a response. Iliyan looked at StarWalker. 'Did you see that?'

*'Does it talk?'* StarWalker nudged the stone.

'Do you talk?' Iliyan asked the stone. It twinkled. She squeezed it in her hand and held it to her heart. 'I wish you could talk to me.'

The stone began to shake and twinkle so violently that it broke apart in Iliyan's hand. A flash of brilliant light blinded Iliyan and StarWalker. They shook their heads and blinked.

StarWalker's eyes adjusted first. *'Look behind you!'* he said.

Iliyan turned around. Standing behind her was a fairy the same size as Iliyan. She had red hair and blue eyes like Iliyan. In fact, she looked just like Iliyan. 'Hello,' said Iliyan, 'who are you?'

'I am Nayili,' said the fairy.

'Where did you come from?' Iliyan couldn't help noticing their dresses were just alike.

'You wished me out of the crystal, silly.' Nayili giggled. StarWalker cocked his head to the side. Nayili's giggle sounded like Iliyan's.

Iliyan looked at the crystal in her hand. It lay in two pieces. The star was gone. 'You're the star?'

'I was.'

'How long have you been in that stone?'

'Oh, it's not what you think.' Nayili lay on the bed and kicked her feet up the wall. 'There's more room in there than you can see. That stone is a doorway to a crystal kingdom. I've lived there for a long time. But, now it's time for me to be with you.'

'Do you know me?' Iliyan asked.

'What do you think?' Nayili flipped over on the bed, hopped onto her knees and looked Iliyan in the face.

'I think it's odd we look just alike. How do we know each other?' Iliyan noticed their boots were the same.

'We come from the same place.' Nayili rolled onto her belly and kicked her feet up behind her.

'Are you from Gaia?'

'No.' Nayili scratched StarWalker's ears.

'I'm sorry. This is my friend, StarWalker, and my name is Iliyan.'

'Yes, I know. I traveled with you from the Fairy Star, remember?'

'Right! I'm sorry. I'm confused. Can you tell me what you meant when you said we come from the same place?'

'The Fairy Star is my home.' Nayili winked at StarWalker.

'I thought you said you were from the Crystal Kingdom?' Iliyan might have been annoyed if she wasn't so confused.

'That's where I've been for some time, but that is not my home. Like you.'

'I'm from the Fairy Star? How do you know that?' Iliyan shook her head.

'Because, I'm your sister.'

Iliyan looked at her double. 'What?'

'We're twins!' Nayili sat up on the bed.

Iliyan's face twisted. 'I'm sorry. I don't remember you.'

'That's okay. You aren't supposed to.'

'What do you mean?' Iliyan put her face in her hands. She wanted to understand what Nayili was saying, but her head was starting to hurt.

'When you chose to go to Gaia, the Council of Twelve decided it would be easier for you to fulfill your mission if you had no memory of home.'

It was true Iliyan had no recollection of any life before Gaia. Her brother and her cousins in the Fairy Glen were the only family she knew. The small fairies she took care of weren't truly her family, but she thought of them that way. She didn't have parents or remember being a child. For all she knew, she'd always been the Fairy Queen.

'Mission?' Iliyan looked up at Nayili.

'You went to Gaia when her fairies needed help. You were one of many who chose to go.'

'What kind of help?'

'Fairy help!' Nayili giggled. 'It was after Gaia had chosen to dream the individual dream.'

'What's that?'

'It was Gaia's wish. Before that time, everything in space experienced itself as One life, One thought, One dream. All the beings felt connected to one another and all of life flowed peacefully, but there was much that could not be experienced. The universe became aware that it had only One thought and, naturally, it wondered if there were other thoughts, other dreams.'

'Other dreams?'

'Gaia loved the universe and when it wondered, she wondered too. She wished to experience her own thoughts and dreams. Her wish was a choice. As she thought her own thoughts, she began an individual life. Because she was a part of the One dream, when she changed, the One dream changed and beings everywhere began dreaming individual dreams. Gaia naturally became the planet of individual experience and beings from all over went to live there. In time, even her name changed.'

'Changed to what?'

'Earth.'

Aneurin pushed open the bedroom door and stopped dead in his tracks, looking back and forth from Iliyan to Nayili. 'Whoa! How'd you do that?'

Startled, Nayili flew up to the ceiling and hovered.

'She's my twin,' Iliyan said. 'This is Nayili.'

'That's so cool!' Aneurin examined Nayili from underneath her.

Slowly, Nayili descended.

Nayili touched the golden tendrils that flew around Aneurin's face. She pouted and looked at her sister. 'I'm so jealous. Only special fairies have dragon friends.'

Aneurin's sudden entrance gave Iliyan a moment to digest this new information. She looked at the delighted dragon, and at StarWalker, and was deeply grateful she had such good friends. In fact, they were such good friends that they could feel Iliyan's confusion and concern. Aneurin was excited, but he sat on the bed and waited to hear what Iliyan had to say. For a moment the room was quiet.

'Nayili was telling us about Earth.' Iliyan finally broke the silence in the room.

'What about it?' Aneurin asked.

'You know about Earth?' Nayili asked.

'I know a little. There are stories about Earth in dragon folklore.'

'Did you know it's also known as Gaia?'

Now Aneurin looked confused. 'No.'

'She was telling us about the individual dream.' Iliyan sat next to Aneurin on the bed.

Nayili continued, enjoying her audience. 'The transition from the One dream to individual dreaming was more difficult than anyone knew it would be. As beings relocated to Gaia and immersed themselves in individual dreaming, the One dream faded for them. That's when the forgetting began. They slowly lost their memory of their connection to all life. They even forgot they'd chosen the individual experience. They felt the pain of being ripped from the One dream, but because they had forgotten, they didn't understand the source of the pain. This frightened them and only made things worse. Gaia tried to absorb the pain, which caused a change in her electromagnetic frequency. The frequency change destabilized her to the point where she thought she might break apart. Her fairies called out to the universe for help to keep her together.'

Iliyan thought about how she'd felt a distant memory of belonging on the Fairy Star; she thought about her own forgetting. It felt just like what Nayili was describing had happened on Gaia.

'Do fairies feel this pain?' Iliyan asked.

'Not usually. The pain is a result of the change in frequency, of the fear and forgetting. Fairies didn't change their frequencies and they don't feel fear.'

'But I forgot, and so did Kelm.'

'That was a choice,' Nayili said.

Nayili's story weighed heavily on Iliyan. She moved onto the floor next to StarWalker and hugged her knees.

Nayili sat next to her. Iliyan compared her hands to her sister's identical pair.

'When we left the Fairy Star I was sure I remembered being there before. So, that part of your story feels right to me. The rest is crazy. Why did the Council choose for me to forget?'

'They didn't choose for you. They were worried. They considered your choice for a long time. Nobody knew what might happen. They knew the mission would be difficult and they thought memories of home would make it even harder for you. They counseled you, but you chose to forget.'

'I wish I could remember that,' Iliyan laughed. Nayili laughed too.

'So because I chose to forget, it wasn't painful for me?'

'When you choose to forget it's like a mental block. The forgetting is complete. There are no nagging thoughts of what you've given up. There was nothing to remind you of home. Gaia became your home.'

'I had a nagging memory when we left the Fairy Star.'

'Yes, because it is time for you to remember.' Nayili squeezed Iliyan's hand.

'Is that why I am in space?'

'Yes. Before you left on your mission, it was agreed that you would return under certain circumstances.'

'What circumstances?'

'Basically, as soon as you were able. We have been unable to communicate with you at all since you left. Your return is a sign that Gaia's frequency is changing again. It is a sign that she is waking from individual dreaming and is choosing to end the cycle of forgetting. The Council of Twelve felt that more help would be needed when Gaia awakened. You agreed to return to get help.'

'What kind of help?'

'Fairy help, silly!' Nayili elbowed Iliyan. 'We hold the frequency of the One dream. We can help Gaia remember.'

'I can't imagine I can help anybody remember anything,' Iliyan sighed.

'Aww. You will. It will come back to you. Be patient.'

Iliyan couldn't help but feel skeptical. 'What about you? Why didn't you go to Gaia with me?'

'I wanted to. We all did. It was to be a great adventure. The Council of Twelve was concerned. They didn't want Mom and Dad to let all three of us go because they didn't know if we would ever return. I agreed to be the one who stayed behind. I did it for Mom and Dad. Later, I chose a mission in the Crystal Kingdom and they let me go. I've been working with the crystals there, just like you work with the fairies on Gaia.'

'And it's okay for you to leave the Crystal Kingdom now?'

'Gaia is considered the most important mission in the universe. I was allowed to work in the Crystal Kingdom only until you needed me.'

'Wait a minute, Mom and Dad?' Iliyan choked.

'King Luran and Queen Velma.'

Iliyan gasped. 'King Luran is my dad?'

'Our dad.'

'I was standing with him. Why didn't he tell me?' Iliyan stood and paced the room. 'Queen Velma? I didn't see a queen!'

'They didn't want you to know just then. That's why I'm telling you now. Mom and Dad thought if you knew you were home you might want to stay and not complete the mission. Mom probably didn't even see you. She always said if you returned, she couldn't bear seeing you leave again. She's missed you and Kelm a lot.'

'I want to go home.' Iliyan looked at her friends. 'I want to see my mother.'

'Of course you do.' Nayili stood in front of Iliyan. 'But first we must return the Capstone Crystal to the Dying Star. The Dying Star is an ancient crystal world that has chosen to move on to its next expression. We removed its Capstone to aide its transition into its next life. Removing the Capstone caused it to begin a death process. There is great crystal knowledge on the Dying Star. Replacing its Capstone will release the crystal knowledge the star holds. The Dying Star has wished to give its knowledge to Gaia. It will help her remember.'

Iliyan grew sad for the first time. She felt heavy. She felt herself missing parents she didn't even remember. She tried to remember what King Luran looked like. Although she'd just met him, she had trouble seeing him in her mind. She wondered about her mother. In all her time on Gaia she had never even wondered about her parents. She knew that fairies had them. She just hadn't thought about her own. She wondered if Kelm thought about them. She couldn't wait to tell Kelm. So many new thoughts swirled inside her.

StarWalker stood up and pressed against Iliyan's leg. She looked at the dog. *'Remember you are here now,'* StarWalker thought to her. Every time she looked at StarWalker, a tremendous gratitude welled up in Iliyan. She hugged her sister. Tears spilled onto her cheeks.

'Thank you for telling me this. Thank you for waiting for me. Thank you for not forgetting. I'm so glad to see you.'

Nayili held Iliyan for a long time. So many times she had missed Iliyan. For a while after Iliyan left for Gaia, Nayili was able to feel her sister through what they had called their 'twin talk.' As children on the Fairy Star, they had always known what the other was thinking and feeling. In time, the connection was lost. She thought about her sister many times. She'd tried and tried to reconnect.

'I could never have forgotten you. I'm so glad you've returned.'

'Dinner!' Sulwyn called up the stairs.

## Chapter 8

# The Abandonment

Isabel sat beaming between Iliyan and Nayili, holding one of their hands in each of hers. Two Iliyans were definitely better than one. 'This is so cool,' she gushed.

'Eat your dinner, Izzy.' Dr Trahern smiled at her. Everyone passed trays and bowls, filling their plates.

'Dr Trahern, do you know anything about Earth?' Iliyan asked.

'Why do you ask?'

'That's where I'm from.'

'Earth? I thought Gaia was your home.'

'Gaia is what I call it.'

'Same planet, two names,' Nayili said. 'It was Gaia when Iliyan went there. Later, its name changed.'

'Earth is the only name dragons know. And yes, Earth is an important part of dragon history, Iliyan. A long time ago, dragons responded to a call for assistance by Earth. It was long after the forgetting and we took the Rainbow Energy because we thought it would help. Many dragons chose to serve and we hoped that Earth would ultimately be a place where dragons could walk among other beings. We were foolish. When we arrived, Earth's beings were lost in fear. We knew there was nothing to fear, but there was no way to communicate that. Violence erupted and when we were attacked, the Rainbow Energy absorbed the anger and fear and exploded, scorching Earth and hurting her beings. Many dragons were killed. We were unable to help. That's when we abandoned her. We knew we could not walk among the beings there and we never intended to hurt them. It was the only thing we could do. We agreed to return if, and when, Earth's beings could remember their connection to all life.'

'It must have been difficult for dragons to leave when you'd had such great expectations,' Nayili said.

Dr Trahern stared at his lap and played with his napkin. 'The Abandonment is still a deep regret to many dragons. Project Earth was the object of considerable dreaming among dragons. Everyone wanted to go. It was considered an honor to serve there.'

'Did you serve, Dad?' Aneurin asked.

'I had not reached the age of decision.' Dr Trahern looked at Iliyan and Nayili. 'That is the age when dragons are allowed to decide for themselves. Until the age of decision, dragon parents make decisions for young dragons. My father and brother went. I stayed on the Dragon World with my mother. My dad came back in the Abandonment. I never saw Art again.'

'Are there still dragons there?' Iliyan asked.

'We don't know.'

Aneurin had stopped breathing. 'I thought Uncle Art died when you were kids.'

'We assumed he had when he didn't return from Earth.' Dr Trahern looked away. When he looked back, his eyes shone with tears. 'I'm sorry I didn't tell you.'

A giant puff of dark maroon smoke billowed out Aneurin's snout. He groaned.

'After the Abandonment, the Elders decided we would not speak of Earth. Partly, they were ashamed. More importantly, they didn't want to keep telling the story of dragon failure. Bad things happen when dragons are angry at themselves, and no one wanted future generations to carry the shame.'

'Does dragon lore say anything about the future of Earth?' Nayili asked.

'Dragons believe that one day a Messenger may come with news that either Earth has been destroyed, or that it is time for dragons to return.' Aneurin recited information he'd learned in school.

Nayili put her hand on Iliyan's shoulder. 'Meet the Messenger,' she announced.

Aneurin gasped. 'Get out of here!' StarWalker lifted his head and cocked it sideways. Everyone looked at Iliyan.

'Well Iliyan, what's the message?' Aneurin planted his elbows on the table, stuck his face on his hands, and stared at Iliyan.

'How should I know? I only recently remembered my name,' Iliyan whined. 'I didn't even know I was the Messenger.' If Nayili had not been holding her by the shoulders, Iliyan would have left the table.

'Has Earth been destroyed?' Isabel asked.

'I don't think so. If Earth was destroyed, why am I here, and where are all the others?'

'Fairy lore doesn't say anything about the destruction of Earth.' Nayili let go of Iliyan. 'Fairies believe that Iliyan would return to get help when Gaia chose to end the cycle of forgetting and return to the One dream. That would mean that its beings would remember their connection to all life. Maybe that's the same as the time of the return of dragons to Earth.'

Dr Trahern thought about what the return of dragons to Earth would mean to all dragons. It is a rare individual who lives long enough to see a prophecy realized. His heart swelled in his chest. 'What a gift your visiting us has been, Iliyan.' Tears welled in his eyes and he rose, stepped away from his chair and walked around the table to Iliyan. She stood up. He put his arms around her and held her. 'Thank you. I have waited a long time to hear this news.'

Although she still didn't understand her role completely, Iliyan felt deeply grateful that she had brought a gift to this family who had done so much to make her feel welcome.

'What now?' Aneurin asked.

'We have to return the Capstone to the Dying Star.' Nayili stood up.

'Right, the Dying Star.' Aneurin grabbed a book from a stack at the end of the table. 'I've been all through my books. I can see the Dying Star clearly in my mind, but I don't know where it is.'

'I know where it is.' Nayili swelled and fluttered her wings. 'I can take you there.'

The mysteries were starting to make sense to Iliyan. 'Of course! King Luran said one of us will know. I thought he meant Aneurin.'

Aneurin restacked his books and gathered plates to return them to the kitchen. 'That's because you and StarWalker can't remember anything, and you didn't know Nayili was inside the pink stone.' Everyone laughed, including Iliyan.

'Just one moment,' Dr Trahern interrupted. 'Iliyan must complete her mission before she leaves the Dragon World.'

'What must I do?' Iliyan asked.

'You must take this message to the Dragon Elders. We must visit them now. And since we will want them to open the gate for us, we must first transmit our intention to them.' The dragon family gathered in a circle in the living room. They all held hands. Dr. Trahern began humming a low growling tone. When he finished Sulwyn carried the tone, then Aneurin, then Isabel. They finished with a loud 'Whoop!' The fairies and StarWalker stared.

'They must know you are coming,' Dr Trahern explained.

'All right. Let's go!' Aneurin made for the door.

'Can I go, Dad?' Isabel asked.

'Dad!' Aneurin complained.

'It's not every day a dragon visits the Elders,' Sulwyn said.

'We'll all go,' Dr Trahern decided. And so the ever-expanding group of adventurers set out: a dragon family of four, twin fairies, and a dog. They left the house and traveled through the rainbow goo past Dr Trahern's office. They passed other dwellings and shops. Dragons everywhere went about their business. Occasionally one would wave, but none were aware of the importance of this day. Dr Trahern nearly exploded with Iliyan's news. He wondered at how different the town would look if everyone knew. There would be dancing in the streets, no doubt.

At the end of town the path turned steep. The travelers flew along, with StarWalker trotting behind. As they traveled up the grade, the light turned a deeper shade of red. Fog gathered. At the top of the steep climb, the travelers stopped at the edge of a great crater. Rainbow flames licked up the center of the crater, nearly to the top. Iliyan looked down at the swirling colors and yawned. Dr Trahern noticed her reaction.

'Quick, before she falls asleep. Let's go. We must walk along the rim until the gate appears,' said Dr Trahern. 'I've heard stories of dragons who walked all day looking for the gate. It's a good thing we announced ourselves first.'

They had circumnavigated the crater once when a fire gate appeared before them. They stepped through the gate into the interior of the crater. It was dark and deep. The rainbow flames plumed up in front of them. A wide path spiraled down the inside wall of the crater. The travelers walked in two's. Dr and Mrs Trahern walked ahead and StarWalker walked behind. Isabel reached for Iliyan's hand. Iliyan squeezed it. They looked at each other and giggled with excitement.

The downward grade leveled off. An immense red dragon met them when they arrived at the end of the path.

'Greetings. I am Fyrank. Are you the Messenger?'

Iliyan stepped forward. 'I am Iliyan from Gaia, also known as Earth.'

'We are pleased you are here. Please follow me.' Fyrank led the group to the center of the crater where Syrra, a large golden dragon with deep green eyes, and Mygera, an emerald dragon with blue eyes, waited. The Elders each took Iliyan's hands in turn and stared into her eyes. Iliyan felt deeply known by each of them. They all gathered in a half circle around a small pedestal upon which a single flame danced.

'Welcome, Messenger. I am Syrra, Keeper of the Rainbow Fire. We have anticipated your arrival for some time. We are the Elders. You have met Fyrank. This is Mygera.'

'Thank you.' Iliyan looked at her feet. Although she had been a queen for as long as she could remember, she had only very recently become a legend of dragon mythology. Dr Trahern touched her shoulder in a fatherly way. Iliyan looked at him and began:

'Respected Elders, I bring news of Earth. It may be time for the return of dragons there. My friends and I are on our way to replace the Capstone in the Dying Star. We believe that doing so may generate a sign that will be visible throughout the universe.'

'What can you tell us about Earth?' Syrra asked. Iliyan spoke of Gaia. Every time she did, her love for the planet grew, as did her desire to return. She didn't feel much like a messenger. All she knew was what happened in the Glen, but she allowed her story to speak for itself.

'Earth is beautiful. The natural world dances in the light from the sun. It sparkles.'

'And what of the Earth beings?' Syrra asked.

'Humans are builders,' explained Iliyan.

'Do you walk among them?'

'Not all of them. Human children visit the Fairy Glen more frequently than ever. Many of them can see us. They sing and play with us. Less and less do we hide ourselves from them.'

'They are not violent?'

'They can be careless, but I have seen no human violence in the Glen.'

'Have you seen any dragons?' Mygera blurted out. Syrra and Fyrank shot looks at her. Mygera apologized. 'I was afraid you would forget to ask.'

'No, Mygera. I haven't seen any dragons.' Iliyan wanted to tell Mygera how small the Glen was, compared to all of Gaia. She wanted to reassure her that there may indeed be dragons somewhere on Gaia, but she stopped herself.

'How is it that you know it is time for the dragons to return?' Syrra asked.

Iliyan was about to say she didn't know, when her sister stepped forward.

'I am Nayili. I come from the Crystal Kingdom. Earth's crystals are transmitting into the universe for the first time since the forgetting. They sing of Gaia's awakening and her desire to remember. If Gaia remembers the One dream, so will all beings who live there. No one can be sure this is the time for the return, but the Messenger is here.' Nayili stepped back to Iliyan's side.

'My friends and I will replace the Capstone in the Dying Star.' Iliyan gestured to the green crystal still strapped to Aneurin. 'I understand that is the next step. The crystal knowledge will be released from the Dying Star. That may generate a sign. We came here to warn you.'

'Thank you, Iliyan.' Syrra bowed. 'Your message is understood. We will watch for the sign. If it is time, the dragons will join you. With great gratitude and joy we will return to Earth. We will be ready.'

'Thank you.' Iliyan and her party bowed to the Dragon Elders. The dragons bowed to one another. Fyrank guided them back to the spiral path to begin their ascent to the crater's rim.

Nayili was the first to arrive on the rim. 'We should leave from here. The rainbow flames will provide a strong catalyst which will help us reach the Dying Star.'

Iliyan turned to Dr Trahern, Sulwyn and Isabel. 'You have been so kind to me.'

'We'll see you again.' Isabel hugged her. 'Won't we, Dad?'

Dr Trahern took Iliyan's hands. 'Iliyan, if it is indeed time for the dragons to return to Earth, you will most certainly see us again. Project Earth was the greatest dragon adventure. The Abandonment left us feeling that we'd failed. We never wanted our story to end there. It is our destiny to return. Good luck.'

Iliyan embraced Dr Trahern and Sulwyn. She hugged Isabel again and winked at her. Secretly, she handed Isabel half of the crystal Nayili emerged from. Iliyan whispered in Isabel's ear. 'Use this crystal to find me if you ever need me. It will link us together.' She kissed the young dragon on the forehead. Iliyan stepped back and saw Aneurin and Dr Trahern embrace. The younger dragon roared to his mother. She roared in return. StarWalker rubbed along the length of the mother dragon.

'You're a good dog.' Sulwyn looked into his eyes. 'We love you.'

Aneurin looked at StarWalker. 'Let's go, Bud!'

StarWalker felt his strong legs flex. He saw Aneurin swoop into the air, the green crystal sparkling on his chest. StarWalker leaped. Iliyan and Nayili flew just behind. They disappeared into the enormous rainbow fire.

# Chapter 9

# Going Deeper

Prince Kelm fell into deep dreaming. The Fairy King visited him there. The Fairy King was one of those dream characters Prince Kelm recognized, but had never met while awake, so far as he knew. The Fairy King said something. Prince Kelm strained, but could not understand him. Kelm awoke to the sound of the Wizard rustling papers on the desk.

'Rise and shine boys. Rise and shine. It is nearly time.'

Nib shook off sleep as he grabbed his quiver and adjusted his clothes. 'Time for what?'

'Gaia awakens. We must go deeper to retrieve the Beacon Stone.'

Nib poked the sleeping Mc*Manigal, who flinched when Nib pinched his nose. The gnome awoke choking and coughing.

'Let's go, Mac.'

'Go where?'

'Deeper,' said Nib. 'Ready?'

'Always ready, Chief,' Mc*Manigal chirped.

'Let's go, Kelm.' Nib shook the Prince's arm.

'I'm awake,' Kelm said, still disturbed by his dream.

The Wizard grabbed his hat and a small scepter with a crystal ball on its end. Then he stepped into the hall.

'We'll take the stairs,' he said and he trotted off. They all descended the main staircase. In the grand entrance hall, at the base of the stairs, the Wizard paused. Binxley stood on the rail. The Wizard motioned for Nib to stand opposite him, Mc*Manigal and Kelm to stand facing each other at his left and right sides. In this way, a circle was formed. The Wizard raised his scepter. 'Incarta relatta sel dim!' he boomed.

The wooden floor of the grand entrance hall melted away, revealing a deep extension of the stairwell. The Wizard ran down the stairs, the black cat at his heels.

When the floor opened up, Nib became more aware of the song of the crystals. Either the song was louder this day or Nib had not paid much attention before. To Nib, the song was so loud he could hardly focus on anything else. It seemed to tell a story of urgency and possibility. It sang of gratitude and love, which nearly overwhelmed him. Nib's feelings were so strong that he stopped on the stairs. The others ran past him. He closed his eyes and took a moment to feel the deep feelings and then, with great love in his heart, he returned that gratitude to the singing crystals. He had come to know the crystal song as the heartbeat of the Earth. He felt his heart in sync with it.

'I am in you and you are in me,' he called. 'Your heart is mine.'

The Wizard paused when he heard Nib's intention. He smiled, and then yelled, 'Nib, snap out of it!'

Nib tore himself away from his moment with the crystal heart of the Earth. He ran to catch up with the Wizard. 'The crystals spoke to me.'

'I heard. Your intention was clear and well spoken, but now it is time for action.' Nib and the Wizard ran side by side.

'Where are we going?'

'Into the heart of the Earth. That is where the Beacon Stone is.'

'What is the Beacon Stone?'

'It is a magnificent Stone that is capable of calling great energy from the universe.'

'Why do we need the Beacon Stone?' Nib asked.

'There will soon be energies available to us from a nearby dying star. Earth can use these energies to further her evolution. The Beacon will assist her.'

'If it is used to call universal energies, why is the Beacon so deep in the Earth?' Nib asked.

'That's an *excellent* question.' The Wizard stopped, delighted by the question. 'The wizards hid it there to protect it. It was known that it would be needed at some future time.' The Wizard grinned and slapped Nib on the back. 'This, my boy, is that time.'

'What's going to happen?'

'If I knew that, I could save us a long journey, and what may be a great amount of work. It's not going to be easy to get that rock to the surface. I only know it is time. And I may be the only one who knows that, so I must act. This may be the great story of my life, Nib. I intend to be in it.'

Nib could see the Wizard was infused with the possibility of his story. His face fairly shone with light. His eyes twinkled with the excitement of adventure as he quickly turned and lead them further down the staircase.

'Why did the wizards hide the Stone?' Nib stumbled on the stair and lost his balance. Prince Kelm grabbed Nib's jacket to steady him.

'The Beacon Stone was considered too powerful to leave on the surface. The Stone magnifies the energy it receives. There was a time when the Earth's human population fell deep into fear, and the fairies became concerned. They were the Stone's keepers. They worried that it would magnify human fear and cause the Earth's destruction. The fairies came to us and asked for help. The wizards chose to place the Stone in the heart of Earth. There it is protected and remains in service to her evolution.'

'How do you know it is time to move it?' Nib asked.

At this, the Wizard stopped dead in his tracks, nearly causing a domino collision on the stairs.

'How did you know to speak your intention at the beginning of our journey?'

'The crystals were singing so loudly to me, I could not do otherwise.'

The Wizard smiled. 'Precisely! Now, may we proceed?'

Nib smiled. He understood. And he appreciated the Wizard's willingness to answer his questions. Nib wanted to ask what all of this had to do with Iliyan, but he understood that some things could only be known when it is their time to be known. There is a time for knowing and there is a time for action. Now was the time for action.

Nib ran abreast of the Wizard. The stairs grew shallower as they ran. Soon they leveled out.

The Wizard slowed. 'I'm looking for a doorway through the rock. It may appear as a single point of light.'

They moved through the tunnel, examining the walls. Mc*Manigal looked up. He saw a point of light. In the dark tunnel, it resembled the first star in the night sky.

'Wizard, might this be it?'

'Good work, Mac!' The Wizard moved into position directly beneath the point of light. He extended his scepter over his head. When he straightened his arm, the tip of the scepter connected to the point of light.

'Sel Ma!' The Wizard held the crystal ball as it lit up. The walls of the tunnel dissolved around the travelers, as if they had never been there.

Nib stood in the tallest chamber he had ever seen. It seemed to extend upward forever. There appeared to be sky above, but it was a faint pinkish-red. The walls were lined with shiny rock, mostly green and black in color. The rock grew all the way up the sides of the chamber. The crystal tone in the chamber was sweet and light, and it pulsed. It made Nib want to whisper.

'Is this the heart of the Earth?'

'Why are you whispering?' Mc*Manigal asked.

'I don't know,' Nib laughed.

'Are you afraid you'll wake the planet?' Mc*Manigal smirked.

'This is the one you should fear waking,' the Wizard whispered. He stood in a corner near the entrance to a cave. Asleep at the mouth of the cave was a giant red and gold dragon. 'He is the Beacon's guardian.'

Mc*Manigal froze. Nib stepped closer. Dragon stories were favorites among elves. For as long as he could remember, he had longed to meet one. Now he stood close enough to feel the dragon's hot breath against his legs. He wished he knew what to do.

Prince Kelm stepped forward. He held his hand in front of his face and breathed into his palm. A yellow and black dragonfly appeared. Its wings glistened as if it had just emerged from its nymph stage. Kelm continued to blow on the creature. The dragonfly moved its wings out and together, practicing for the first time.

'Ingling!' Prince Kelm said and he blew on the dragonfly. The dragonfly flew toward the dragon.

Prince Kelm breathed into his palms again. A pomegranate appeared. He stepped forward and placed the fruit in front of the dragon's nose. Then Prince Kelm stepped back. He motioned for the others to do the same.

The Wizard was the only one of them who had ever met a dragon. He knew that waking a dragon could be dangerous business. Prince Kelm used his finger in the air in front of him. In this way he directed the dragonfly's route to the dragon's ear. Prince Kelm whispered. The Wizard understood Kelm was speaking to the dragon through the dragonfly. This was powerful magic. The Wizard was impressed. He'd never met a dragon whisperer.

The dragon stirred. The Wizard stepped back squarely on Mc*Manigal's toe. Mc*Manigal flinched, but did not speak. All eyes were on Kelm and the dragon.

Kelm walked silently back and forth in front of the dragon's nose. In this way the dragon could adjust to Kelm's scent. The dragon stirred again.

Prince Kelm directed the dragonfly to land on the dragon's nose. The dragon opened one eye and then closed it sleepily. He opened it again. He eyed the dragonfly. When he opened his second eye, he saw past the dragonfly to the pomegranate. He blinked to focus his eyes when he saw Prince Kelm standing just beyond the fruit. The dragon pulled himself up to his full height and roared. Fire blew from his nose. Luckily, the fire rose straight up. Kelm felt the heat. He knew the dragon could have incinerated him if he chose to. Not being incinerated in this moment was good fortune. The roar had been a warning.

The dragon snorted; one eye on Kelm and one on the shiny red fruit. He stood several times Kelm's height.

Kelm stood silent. For every hero, there is a moment when he questions the wisdom of his actions. This moment comes after the hero has waded out into the deep waters of his own adventure with great forward thrust, not looking back. Suddenly, he realizes he can no longer see land. That's when the hero wonders if his next move will be his last. This thought is almost always followed by the acknowledgement that it is too late to turn back. For a moment, Kelm wondered at the wisdom of his own boldness. He laughed to himself. Then he toned a series of notes. Many of the notes were harsh, as if he were singing off-key. He finished with a forceful growl.

The dragon picked up the fruit and moved to expose the cave's entrance. With one claw he sliced open the pomegranate and tasted a seed. Be breathed out a purr, and then selected another seed. Prince Kelm looked at the others.

'I believe we have been granted passage.'

'My goodness man!' Mc*Manigal breathed for the first time since the dragon awoke. 'How'd you manage that?'

The Wizard walked up and put his hand on the Prince's shoulder.

'How did you do that?' Nib asked.

'I'm not sure. Just lucky, I guess.'

'That wasn't luck.' The Wizard slapped Kelm's shoulder. 'That was fine magic and great skill. I've heard that fairies can be skilled with dragons, but I've never heard of or seen anything like that. Top job, Prince.'

'Thank you. After you.' Kelm motioned past the dragon, toward the cave.

'Right!' Nib stopped and stared at Kelm. He looked at the dragon. He truly was a magnificent creature. Nib hadn't been this excited, ever. 'Impressive!'

'Come along!' The Wizard ran through the cave entrance.

Nib, Mc*Manigal and Prince Kelm followed the Wizard inside the cave. In the cave sat an immense rock, green with brown veins. It was smooth, and nearly as large as the dragon.

'Oh my,' said Nib, 'that's a rock! How are we going to move it?'

They walked in a line around the rock, examining it.

'What about dematerialization?' Prince Kelm asked.

'You mean fairy style?' Mc*Manigal laughed. 'How can we be sure it will ever re-materialize?'

'I'm afraid magic is out.' The Wizard walked around the rock. 'Some rocks can be dematerialized, but not this one. This one has to be moved as it is. Earth depends on its energy. She won't take kindly to its sudden disappearance.'

'Let me try.' Mc*Manigal wedged himself under the rock at the side. The rock tipped slightly. Mc*Manigal worked himself to the center of the underside of the rock. Once there, he raised the rock up on his back with a groan. He attempted a step and was nearly crushed. Nib and the Wizard quickly pushed the rock so it tipped off his back. Mc*Manigal crawled out.

'I can lift it, but I won't get far with it.'

The Wizard knew of the legendary strength of gnomes, but Mc*Manigal's demonstration took him by surprise. 'I have to say that I could not have assembled a finer group than this group here if I'd designed each of you myself, but there is only one who can move that rock.'

Mc*Manigal and Prince Kelm looked at Nib.

'Don't look at me. I don't have any hidden skills.'

'No, not Nib,' the Wizard said, 'the dragon. Kelm, do you think you can ask him to take this rock to the surface?'

'I can try.'

'You must tell him that the fairies need the rock returned. Surely he is aware they were its original keepers. Tell him that the time of the return of dragons to the Earth may be at hand. If he remembers anything he will understand this.'

Prince Kelm left the cave and returned to the dragon. The pomegranate was nearly gone.

'Dragon!' Kelm spoke in a dragon growl (which is impossible to type with only twenty-six available letters). 'I am Prince Kelm of the Fairy Realm. I offer the greatest fairy gratitude to you for your service to the Beacon Stone. I am here because the fairies are in need of the Stone's return to the surface. I have been sent to retrieve it, but I need your help. I have been told that it may be nearly time for the dragons to return to Earth.' The dragon finished the pomegranate. 'Thank you, dragon.' Prince Kelm finished.

'I am Arthmael,' the dragon replied. 'Why do the fairies need the Stone?'

'There is a star that is dying in space. It is believed that the star holds energies that will be transmitted to Earth. The Stone is needed to transform the incoming energy so Earth can use it.'

'What is this of the return of dragons to the Earth?' Arthmael swished his long tail along the ground.

The Wizard stepped next to Kelm. 'Earth wishes to awake from her dream and end the cycle of forgetting. The fairies wish to call the dragons to assist. The Beacon Stone is needed for the communication. It will redirect the energy of the Dying Star out into the universe to call the dragons.'

Arthmael cocked his head sideways. He was thinking.

'If it turns out we are wrong, I will personally see to it that the Stone is returned to your cave,' Prince Kelm offered his assurance.

Arthmael stood and faced Prince Kelm. He bowed, and then roared, 'I am honored to assist the fairies.'

Kelm and the Wizard followed the dragon into the cave. He stepped over the Stone. Everyone backed up to the wall to give the dragon room. Grasping the Stone in his strong legs, Arthmael used his wings to hop the Stone out of the cave and into the center chamber. He extended his wings fully and flapped. He flew straight up, the Stone secure in his grip. He made it clear he intended to fly up and out the top.

Nib called to the Earth. 'With great gratitude we gladly return the Beacon Stone to its place on the surface. Thank you. I am in you as you are in me,' he said.

Prince Kelm flew up and straddled the neck of the dragon. Arthmael lowered himself back into the chamber.

'Jump on!' Kelm said.

Nib moved so fast he tripped. He clamored up the great beast's back. The Wizard followed him. Without even looking, Nib knew Mc*Manigal had hesitated.

'C'mon, Mac! You conquered your fear of heights, remember.'

'It's my fear of fire that's got me now, Nib.' Mc*Manigal trembled as he mounted the dragon. He sat behind the grinning Nib, who sat behind the grinning Wizard, who sat behind the grinning Kelm. Each of them was sure this dragon would deliver them to their individual destinies. Mc*Manigal wasn't as confident his destiny was a good one.

'Ready, Bud?' Nib asked.

'Always ready!' the gnome croaked.

## Chapter 10

# The Dying Star

Iliyan looked back at Dr Trahern and Sulwyn. She blew Isabel a kiss and leaped from the rim of the crater into the rainbow fire. Nayili was at her side. Rainbow colors swirled around them. Iliyan felt as though she were dissolving. She expected to feel the sensation of falling, but instead felt suspended on air. She bobbed up and down as the flames pushed her and danced around her. She felt she could stay in this place forever, when suddenly she found herself flying through space, on her sister's heels. She saw Aneurin in the distance behind her, but she didn't see StarWalker.

StarWalker touched off a moon and sprang into the air behind Iliyan. She was hard to see so he kept a picture of her in his mind. As they approached the Dying Star, Iliyan flew to Nayili's side. She was amazed at how smart her sister was.

'How did you know where to go?'

'I didn't know. It's a feeling.' Nayili flew closer to the star. She was looking for something. 'In the Crystal Kingdom I learned that everything that has form is held together by an electromagnetic grid structure. I learned how to see the grids. The Dying Star looks like a light pattern of mostly triangles that are all connected. There are areas where the angles are bright and strong and areas where the lines are broken and disconnected. Even in parts that are broken and disconnected, there can still be light in the grid there. There are other areas where there is no light and no gridlines, areas of complete darkness. These are voids. When the Capstone was removed, it left a void. It was this void that caused the star to leak energy.'

'Why was the Capstone removed?'

'The star requested it as part of its evolution. It chose to die in its current form in order to be born into a new experience. Once it has given all its energy to Gaia, the grid will go dark and the star will no longer appear in this place in the sky. There is great wisdom in this star. It chose to give its wisdom and energy to assist Gaia's evolution. One day, Gaia will be a star like this.'

'Where will this star be then?' Iliyan couldn't imagine that such a large bright body could just disappear from the sky.

'Oh, it will still be here, just not in this dimension of space. Although you cannot see her, you are also very close to Gaia. You have been all along.'

'But I am in space.'

'So is Gaia, silly.' Nayili giggled. 'That you cannot see her does not mean she's not here.'

'When will I see her?'

'Soon. We're getting close.' Nayili spotted a dark part of the grid about the size of the stone. 'Aneurin,' she yelled, 'bring the stone in here.' Aneurin hovered near Nayili with the stone. Nayili pointed to the dark hole. 'Move above us and drop the stone into place there.'

Aneurin flew up above Nayili. He looked down. He saw only hot white light. Nayili untied the vines that held the stone. Aneurin dropped the stone when he heard Nayili say, 'Now!' The stone dropped into the white light and stopped in the dark hole.

Iliyan and Nayili watched the stone settle into place. The stone lit from within. The dark void filled with bright white light. The light expanded, increasing the brightness of the star by many times.

'What's happening?' Iliyan asked.

'The stone is accelerating the star's energy. We should go. We don't have much time now.' Nayili flew away from the star.

Iliyan looked around. The noise from the Dying Star was loud. She flew close to Aneurin and yelled. 'Where is StarWalker?'

Aneurin looked around for his friend. 'I don't know. I thought he was right behind me.'

'I'm going to find him.' Iliyan flew through the loud white light. She thought his name over and over and she felt a pull in her heart. StarWalker had been beside her the entire time she had been in space and she felt lost without him. She flew into the impossibly bright star and found him standing on a solid piece of the grid.

'There you are! I've been looking for you.' Iliyan landed on the grid next to StarWalker and hugged him.

*I landed on this piece and I can't leap from here.*

'Are you injured?' Iliyan felt each of StarWalker's strong legs.

*No. I feel like I'm too heavy to jump.*

'Hmm.' Iliyan stood and looked around. 'It must be something about the grid.' Iliyan secretly tried her wings. She easily lifted off. She folded her wings and touched back down. StarWalker watched Aneurin fly up.

'Don't land here, Aneurin,' Iliyan called out. 'We're stuck. Go get Nayili, would you?'

'Sure!' Aneurin flew off.

*'You're stuck, too?'* StarWalker looked at Iliyan.

'Yes,' Iliyan lied. She sat down next to StarWalker and put her head on his back. She thought about the Fairly Dusty Moon. 'I'm so glad you found me on that moon.'

*'I'm so glad you were there to be found. In all the places I've ever been, and of all the things I've ever found, you're the best.'*

A loud crack and a low rumble came from inside the star. Another followed it.

Nayili flew up. 'You're stuck?'

'Yes. It's very dense here. Neither one of us can take off.'

Nayili watched the grid break up around Iliyan and StarWalker. Curious, she touched down on the surface. Immediately she moved her wings and easily lifted off. She eyed Iliyan, who sat with her arms around StarWalker's neck. The star cracked and groaned.

Aneurin was getting anxious. 'This doesn't look good, Bud. What do we do?'

'You two get to safety,' said Iliyan. 'We'll keep trying.'

Neither Aneurin nor Nayili wanted to leave them there. 'Keep trying to get off.' Nayili looked at Iliyan. 'As the star's field breaks up, there may be an opportunity for you.'

'We'll catch up to you. Go! Now!'

A loud crack was heard and large pieces of the star fell off and flew out into space. StarWalker tried to jump again.

'*Impossible.*' StarWalker shook his head in disbelief. '*It's like I'm made of lead.*'

Nayili and Aneurin moved out of the way of the star's flying debris. Nayili was torn. She wondered what would happen to the sister she'd only just been reunited with. Nayili knew that Iliyan could lift off the star if she wanted to. She understood Iliyan didn't want to leave StarWalker alone to an uncertain fate, but she wanted to know her sister would be all right. Nayili knew she was being selfish. She'd watched Iliyan leave once before and she didn't want to experience that again.

Aneurin thought about his friend. Dragons do not worry, but they love deeply. He repeated the same thought over and over. *I'll see you soon, Bud.*

The star split open. Two hot white beams of light shot from the Capstone Crystal and traveled straight out into space. From a distance, one could see that one light beam traveled to the Fairy Star and the other traveled to the Dragon World.

On the Dying Star, Iliyan held onto StarWalker as he tried to leap again.

'*You try,*' StarWalker said.

'No. I'm staying with you.' Iliyan held on tight.

What was left of the star split into two pieces, and the surface they sat on gave way. StarWalker and Iliyan fell as a single unit and landed on the Capstone Crystal.

Underneath them, the crystal glowed brilliant white and shook. Iliyan wondered how the crystal had been able to hold such an intense energy inside it. All around them, the star broke up in a cacophony of light and sound as the crystal vibrated beneath them.

A moment later, the vibrations slowed. Iliyan watched the light beams fade as the Dying Star spent its energy. She wondered where the light went and if one of the destinations was Earth. When the Dying Star went dark, a rainbow emanated from one of the destination points and traveled through space to the other destination point, linking them.

'Look!' Iliyan turned StarWalker's face toward the rainbow. *Perhaps it is the time for the return of dragons to the Earth,* she thought.

'Indeed,' StarWalker thought in return.

Iliyan thought about her adventure, about the dear dragon family that felt like her own. She thought about Aneurin, who was smart and brave and didn't mind remembering everything for everyone. She thought about Nayili, the twin sister she didn't remember. How smart Nayili was. Iliyan thought about her father, who she'd only seen briefly. She thought about her brother. *I must remember to tell Kelm everything when I get back.* Finally Iliyan thought about her mother. She wondered if she would ever see her again. With each thought, Iliyan's heart felt like it grew larger in her chest. She looked at StarWalker and she thought her heart might explode. She grabbed his face in her hands, and stared into his eyes.

'You are such a good dog,' she said and she kissed him smack on the nose.

Iliyan could not have known that those are the words that every dog longs to hear. StarWalker would never forget this moment, as much because of what happened before it, as what happened next.

The Capstone was utterly silent. Iliyan and StarWalker looked at each other. Then, in one horrendous rumble, it blew into a million pieces and sent Iliyan and StarWalker hurtling through space. Iliyan tried to hold onto StarWalker, but the force of the blast separated them. She watched StarWalker fall. She wondered if her heart had exploded, too. Falling through space, she felt deep love and gratitude for his friendship. Then, she blacked out.

# Chapter 11

# Sacred Geometry

Prince Kelm navigated Arthmael through the Inner Earth labyrinths, up through tunnels and into caverns, swooping and turning, rising and falling. Mc*Manigal grew sick to his stomach and dreamed of the end of his flying days. Prince Kelm saw a spot of blue high above and flew toward it. They broke through the relative darkness of Earth's heart center and onto the False Surface. The False Surface looks exactly like Surface Earth, but it is in the inner realms and so has no sun that rises or sets. They flew past mountains and along a river, to an immense grassy plain with wildflowers, rolling hills in the distance, and forests beyond that. Kelm landed near the forest.

The Wizard scrambled down the spikes on the dragon's tail. 'Let me see if I can figure out where to go next.' He jumped off and walked back and forth near the forest. Occasionally he stood perfectly still, listening. A gentle wind rustled the leaves of the trees as the Wizard concentrated. The wind grew stronger. 'Aha! I get it.' The Wizard pointed a finger straight up and looked at Prince Kelm. 'I'll be right back.' He ran into the forest.

Nib jumped off the dragon. He ran into the forest behind the Wizard. The further in he ran, the darker it became.

'Wizard! Can you hear me?' Nib listened. Leaves rustled. Nib heard sticks breaking on the forest floor behind him. He turned, expecting the Wizard. An immense tree stood where there had been nothing a moment ago.

'Whoa!' Nib breathed as he watched a face appear in the bark of the tree.

'Good day.' The tree smiled.

Nib felt nervous. 'I am Nib. I'm looking for the Wizard. We are on a quest to find the Fairy Queen.'

'Are you looking for the Wizard or are you looking for the Fairy Queen?'

'Both, but I know the Wizard is in this forest. I watched him run in here a moment ago. As for Iliyan, I have no idea where she is.'

'Hmm,' the tree grumbled. 'Have you looked in the Glen?'

'She and her brother went missing from the Glen. We found the Prince in the Himalayas.'

'Yes, I know all that,' said the tree.

'How do you know?'

'I heard it from the trees in Fairy Meadows.'

'You talk to trees in the Himalayas?' Nib scratched his head.

'I talk to trees everywhere. We are all connected. Oh, I have something for you.'

'What is it?'

'It's up in my branches. You have to climb up and get it.'

Nib was an excellent tree climber. He hugged the tree and jigged up to its lowest branch. From there he jumped and caught the next branch, swung his body and reached with his legs, flipping himself up to the next layer of branches. When he was almost near the top, the tree shook one of its branches.

'There! Go out on that limb.'

Nib straddled the limb and inched his way out. A bunch of arrows, tied together with a vine, rested at the end of the limb. Nib grabbed the bunch and scooted back to a strong part of the limb. He steadied himself and examined the arrows. They each bore the symbol Nib carved into the arrows he made.

'Hey, these are my arrows.'

'Indeed.'

'Where did you get them?'

'They came from all the places you ever lost an arrow. I understand you're a pretty good shot. Some trees don't mind being pierced. These arrows are from the ones that do mind. They move out of the way.'

'Move out of the way?' Nib was excited. 'You mean those shots were good?' Nib silently recalculated his average.

'I can't speak for all of them, but most of them, yes. That's my understanding. Some of the trees had to move pretty swiftly to get out of the way. It's a good thing you wear a blindfold. We're not supposed to allow anyone to see us moving about. The trees love to tell the stories. They call it Nib's Aim Game. It's a badge of honor among the trees to have dodged one of your arrows.'

Nib didn't know what to say. His mother had called his game 'silly'.

He had thought it was just a game he played by himself. It was a curious feeling to learn he didn't play alone.

'Here comes the Wizard.' The tree shook its branches. Nib leaped down the branches close to the trunk.

'Thanks.' Nib patted the trunk and jumped to the ground.

'You're welcome. And good luck with the Fairy Queen and your Aim Game.'

Nib looked up at the tree. He was sure it winked at him. He winked back. The Wizard ran up behind him, panting.

'There you are,' said Nib.

The Wizard bent over and held his knees in his hands to catch his breath. 'Come now. It is time. The trees revealed the exact location where we are to place the Beacon Stone. It's in the middle of Iliyan's Glen. Let's go!' The Wizard ran past Nib toward the meadow.

Nib tucked the arrows into his quiver and ran after the Wizard. The Wizard ran up the dragon's back and spoke to Prince Kelm. 'You must get the Stone to the Fairy Glen quickly.'

Prince Kelm spoke the command in dragon. Nib had barely jumped onto the dragon's back when it took flight. He scrambled up while the dragon flew.

Prince Kelm navigated Arthmael to a gate that led to Surface Earth. They swooped through the gate and onto Surface Earth. Kelm looked around, but he didn't see the Glen. He knew it would be hard to find by looking. He decided to seek its location in his heart. He closed his eyes and saw it in his mind. He saw Iliyan and the other fairies. When he opened his eyes, he knew exactly where it was. He turned the dragon toward the setting sun. They flew high over houses and trees. He saw the lake first. He flew Arthmael in a circle around the Glen and commanded the dragon to land.

It was clear the fairies had not been expecting them. Dozens of fairies froze at the sight of the dragon. If any of them had seen a dragon before, they didn't remember it. Fairies cannot freeze for long and within a few moments there was such a ruckus around the dragon that he was barely visible. Mc*Manigal climbed down, vowing never to fly again. Nib and the Wizard followed him. Prince Kelm remained atop Arthmael and greeted the fairies.

The Wizard strode around the dragon, examining the ground. He looked at the trees that surrounded the fairy ring. Arthmael had landed in the center of the ring.

'This is perfect,' the Wizard yelled to Prince Kelm. 'Set it down here.'

Kelm commanded the dragon to drop the Stone. They were surrounded by fairies, as delighted to see the missing Prince, as they were to meet the dragon. Arthmael enjoyed the attention. He was watching a small fairy fly around his snout when he heard Prince Kelm's command. He let go of the crystal and stepped aside. The fairies swarmed the Stone.

Nib found Eritha next to a tree. 'Thank you!' He bowed slightly and walked over to her.

'Thank you.' Eritha bowed her head in return. 'We have been preparing a celebration. It has kept us busy.'

'Excellent.'

'What happens next?'

'I'm not sure. The Wizard said we had to bring the Beacon Stone.'

'I know this Stone.' Eritha walked into the ring and around the Stone. 'I remember my father was on the team that requested its protection. It is very powerful.' She put her hand on the top of the Stone. 'It is good to have it home.' She looked at Nib. 'Did you find Iliyan?'

'No.' Nib wondered how the fairies would feel when they realized he had failed to find their Queen.

'Well it seems there's only one thing to do.' Eritha lifted her skirts slightly and danced in a small circle.

'What's that?' Nib walked behind her.

'Celebrate Prince Kelm's return! Can you play your pipe?'

Nib pulled his pipes from his pocket and began to play.

'Today we celebrate!' Eritha called out. 'Today we celebrate the return of Prince Kelm and the Beacon Stone to the Fairy Glen. Today we celebrate the coming of the dragon!' All the fairies cheered and danced around the Glen. They danced around the Stone, around Prince Kelm, and around the dragon. The Wizard danced too. Mc*Manigal tried to slip out, but Nib caught up to him and engaged him in a jig. There was bowing and skipping and much merriment.

The fairies dancing near the lake noticed it first. As they darted in and out of the water for fun, they noticed when they went into the water, they came out dizzy. They spun when they flew out. It was fun. As they played in the dizzying water, a lavender light settled on the Glen. Along with the light came a tone. At first it seemed the tone came from Nib's pipe, but it sweetly sang a single pitch and it grew louder. Some of the fairies dancing near the Beacon Stone knew the Stone was singing the note.

Now if one stood a distance from the Fairy Glen, one could clearly see two beams of light, one green and one red, shining into the Fairy Glen from space. But in the Glen itself, one could only hear the sweet note and see the faintest lavender light.

# Chapter 12

# Return to Earth

The Fairy Star vibrated and emanated a verdant green light that sang a vibrant note. All of the Star's crystals twinkled. King Luran gathered stones. He grabbed his crystal wand and headed for the Council Chambers. He found the Council convened at the stone ring, his wife, Queen Velma, at its head.

'Are you ready?' The King joined his wife.

'Oh, yes!' Queen Velma shook with excitement. 'I can hardly wait.'

King Luran tapped his crystal wand lightly on the ring. Its pinging sound quieted the room.

'Today is the day we celebrate our reunion with our friends, the joyful completion of the mission to Gaia, and the end of the time of forgetting. Many sacrifices have been made. Today we travel to Gaia to witness her awakening from individual dreaming, and we celebrate her return to the One dream. Our friends have assisted her development, unaware of their true home. Today we greet the many we have missed. What a joyful day!' The Council cheered and the crystal walls of the chamber sparkled.

'The return of the Capstone Crystal to the Dying Star has assisted the Star's passage into its next highest frequency. In so doing, the Star as we have known it is gone. Its final and significant gifts of power, wisdom and energy were transmitted here and to the Dragon World. When the rainbow connected our worlds, we began transmitting the Star's light to Gaia. A magnificent energetic triangulation has resulted, and it is through this triangulation that we will travel to Earth. It is time.'

King Luran took his wife's hand and bowed. Together, they led the procession out of the Council Chambers.

- - -

On the Dragon World, the Elders sang as the rainbow fire glowed. The red light from the fire grew to a deep intensity around the planet and filled the stream of light that connected it to Earth.

'It is time!' Syrra announced and she, Fyrank, and Mygera roared a mighty dragon sound and took flight. From all corners of the Dragon World, dragons lifted off.

At Aneurin's house, Isabel nervously flittered about, knocking things over. She gathered her belongings.

'Isabel,' Sulwyn tried to calm her young daughter, 'you don't need all those things. It's just a short trip. We'll be coming right back.'

'Are you sure Mom? I've heard dragons talk of staying on Earth.'

'Yes dear, some will choose to stay. And once you reach the age of choice, you may choose to travel to any number of worlds, but for now you will stay with us and we will be returning home.'

'What about Aneurin, Mom?'

'He's old enough to choose for himself, dear. Are you ready?'

Isabel squeaked an unusually high-pitched response for a dragon and grabbed the pink crystal Iliyan had given her. They all met at the door.

'Let's go!' Dr Trahern opened the door and they stepped out into the street and lifted off in time to see the Dying Star explode.

'I hope they're okay.' Isabel hovered and stared at the dark hole in space that now existed where the star had been only moments before. She squeezed the crystal in her hand.

'I hope so, too,' her parents spoke at the same time.

Into the red stream the dragon family flew. It was upon these powerful streams of light that the fairies and dragons traveled to Earth. Dragons poured into the red stream from their world, and fairies poured into the green stream from their world. As the streams merged, they mingled. Fairies squealed and dragons roared. Everyone was excited.

- - -

StarWalker watched Iliyan fall through space. He did everything he could to stay close to her as they fell into the light streams of the triangulation. Surrounded by deep lavender light, Iliyan stirred. She opened her eyes and saw StarWalker upside down above her.

'Are you okay?' She fluttered her wings and regained control of her falling form. She took flight, slowing her descent. StarWalker dropped past her like a stone. She had regained control precisely at the last moment.

A sharp golden flash of light blinded her. Iliyan fluttered her wings and hung in space for a moment. She blinked. Suddenly she saw the throngs of fairies and dragons around her in the energy stream. She blinked again. There was a loud splash.

StarWalker crashed into the lake. He found himself underwater. He saw fairies flitting about and he moved his strong legs. Glad the sensation of falling was over, he swam in the water, which felt like leaping through space. He bobbed to the surface. He was in the center of a beautiful blue lake. At the lake's edge everything was green. Fairies and dragons crowded the sky above him.

In the Glen the crystal tone rose to a crescendo. A brilliant flash of golden light exploded. Its afterglow hung on the horizon. The splash brought the dancing to a halt and everyone rushed to the lake. As Nib's eyes adjusted, he saw a white object moving in the center of the lake.

'Look! It's a dog!'

As they watched the dog swim in circles in the center of the lake, fairies and dragons became visible in the space all around them. The Glen fairies rushed to greet them. StarWalker was relieved to see Iliyan appear above him.

*'I'm swimming.'* He paddled along.

'Yes, in circles.' Iliyan giggled.

*'It's marvelous.'*

'Follow me to the shore!' Iliyan flew in the direction of Nib and the Wizard. She touched down beside them. She saw the beautiful Glen, alive with prancing fairies and glowing in lavender light.

'I have you to thank for this,' Iliyan said to Nib.

'Not just me.' Nib blushed. 'It was a team effort.'

'Thank you.' Tears dropped onto Iliyan's cheeks.

'We're so glad you're home.' The Wizard beamed and blushed all at the same time.

StarWalker stepped onto the shore.

'Hey, that's the dog from my dream,' Nib whispered to the Wizard.

'Of course it is.' The Wizard laughed.

Drenched, StarWalker had never felt so heavy. Instinctively, he began what was the first and most delicious shake of his life. It began as a tickle at the tip of his nose and rippled down his body to the end of his tail, in waves he could not control. Water droplets flew off him in every direction. When it stopped, he shook again.

Iliyan hugged him. 'This is the Glen. We made it. I'm so happy. I have so much to show you!' Iliyan continued speaking quickly, in the short sentences fairies use then they're excited, as a swarm of small Glen fairies gathered around StarWalker. Many of them landed on his nose, which tickled, causing him to shake some more. He greeted each one. They introduced themselves in alphabetical order.

'Hi I'm Alex.'

'Hi I'm Alyssa.'

'Hi, I'm Ariane.'

StarWalker heard so many names, he couldn't possibly remember them all.

Aneurin flew into the Glen. He spotted Arthmael and landed near him, Nayili at his side. They walked toward the crowd that surrounded the immense red and gold dragon.

'That dragon looks like me,' Aneurin said to Nayili.

'And you look like him.'

As they walked closer, Arthmael growled a greeting.

'Uncle Art?' Aneurin howled and the two dragons danced on their hind legs in circles around each other. Other dragons gathered around. Dr Trahern swooped overhead and dropped on top of his brother, tackling him to the ground. They rolled in the Fairy Glen, howling and hugging.

Prince Kelm flew off to safety before the rolling began. Thinking she was Iliyan, he landed next to Nayili.

'I have something to tell you.' He prepared to confess his bad magic.

Nayili grabbed her brother and hugged him. 'Oh Kelm,' she cried. 'It will have to wait. Our parents are here.'

'What?' Kelm sputtered as Nayili grabbed his arm and took off. She flew him to where King Luran and Queen Velma were greeting the Glen fairies. From a distance, Iliyan saw her mother hug her brother and she flew to join her family. She hugged her mother for a long time. Prince Kelm looked first at Nayili, and then at Iliyan.

'What the...?' His face screwed up in confusion.

'Kelm has something to tell you, Iliyan.' Nayili giggled.

'Yes?' Iliyan wiped a tear away and sniffed.

Kelm addressed both his sisters at once. 'I'm sorry I made you disappear. I was practicing bad magic.'

'Bad magic?' Iliyan and Nayili interrupted him. They looked at each other and laughed in stereo. It was a beautiful laugh that hushed the Glen. The sound of the Fairy Queen's laughter is the favorite sound of fairies. When they heard it, they realized Iliyan had returned.

The high-pitched 'Eeeee' sound of pure fairy joy began with one small fairy and grew as it rolled through the Glen. The 'Eeeee' grew so loud that StarWalker could not resist. He pointed his nose at space and howled a bright, clear tone, as close as he could sing to the pitch of the 'Eeeee'. A moment later the dragons joined in. Unable to reach so high a pitch, they roared their own harmonic note.

The light energy from the triangulation and the ecstatic symphony rose from the Glen and enveloped the Earth. Gaia's heart awakened and she felt the love of the One dream all around and through her. Her heart joined the chorus. The forgetting was forgotten and in that moment, fear and pain ceased to exist on Earth.

## About the Author

Alyson Budde lives in the fairy-rich Pacific Northwest, United States. She dreamed of reading this book when she was very young. Her great joy has been the journey that has allowed her dream to come true. Now, she is certain the very best dreams are those dreamed in childhood.